D1013350

Perfect Phrases for Managing Your Small Business

Also available from McGraw-Hill

Perfect Phrases for Performance Reviews by Douglas Max and Robert Bacal

Perfect Phrases for Performance Goals by Douglas Max and Robert Bacal

Perfect Solutions for Difficult Employee Situations by Sid Kemp

Perfect Phrases for Customer Service by Robert Bacal

Perfect Phrases for Business Proposals and Business Plans by Don Debelak

Perfect Phrases for Meetings by Don Debelak

Perfect Phrases for the Sales Call by William T. Brooks

Perfect Phrases for Lead Generation by William T. Brooks

Perfect Phrases for Sales and Marketing by Barry Callen

Perfect Phrases for Executive Presentations by Alan Perlman

Perfect Phrases for College Application Essays by Sheila Bender

Perfect Phrases for Writing Grant Proposals by Beverly Browning

Perfect Phrases for Real Estate Agents and Brokers by Dan Hamilton

Perfect Phrases for Managing Your Small Business

Robert Bacal
Nancy Moore

New York Chicago San Francisco Lisbon
London Madrid Mexico City Milan New Delhi
San Juan Seoul Singapore Sydney Toronto

1 2 3 4 5 6 7 8 9 0 FGR/FGR 0 1 0 9 8

ISBN: 978-0-07-160052-1
MHID: 0-07-160052-3

This is a *CWL Publishing Enterprises Book* produced for McGraw-Hill by CWL Publishing Enterprises, Inc., Madison, Wisconsin, www.cwlpub.com.

McGraw-Hill books are available at special quantity discounts to use as premiums and sales promotions, or for use in corporate training programs. To contact a representative, please visit the Contact Us pages at www.mhprofessional.com.

Contents

Contents

Contents

Contents

Contents

Contents

Contents

Preface

There are three kinds of people. Some people should never attempt to build, own, or operate a small business because they are temperamentally unsuited to the task, or they lack the skills and knowledge and have no desire to learn them. Other people are very well suited to owning or managing a small business and recognize the need for continuous learning in order to succeed. These are the people who do succeed. Finally, there are the people who want to get rich fast and grasp at anything that offers false promises, often involving scams that victimize others.

This book is for you if you need to find out if you are suited to owning and running a small business. It's for you if you want to learn how to succeed in small business. It's NOT for you if you want to make a quick buck or take advantage of others.

Small businesses that last are built on fundamentally sound ideas. They are well planned. They have well-thought-out business and marketing strategies. They are properly funded.

Perhaps the most important part is that businesses built to last are owned and operated by people who want to learn, who are realistic and honest about themselves, and who understand the commitment needed to succeed.

This book will help you learn about yourself so you can decide if small business is for you. We'll walk you through the process of making initial business decisions, help you develop a business plan, and help you present it to people who can further or impede your endeavor.

We'll help you manage yourself as a small business person, something that's absolutely critical to remaining fresh and creative, and we'll help you with personnel issues, hiring, employee orientation, leadership and much more.

We'll provide you with ideas on developing a marketing plan and strategy, and we'll describe the methods by which you can implement them. And of course no marketing efforts can succeed without knowing how to make the sale. We'll cover that.

The Unique Format

In keeping with other books in the Perfect Phrases series, the majority of the content of this book consists of either phrases or questions. In some cases, these phrases or questions are meant to be used with another person. So, for example, if you are talking to a banker about financing, we provide phrases and questions to use with the banker to decide whether to continue business with him or her. As another example, we provide questions and statements you might use to mediate between two employees who are in conflict.

However, we take the phrases idea further. Small business success is about making the correct decisions for the situation. This book helps you *think through* difficult small business problems and issues by giving you questions to ask yourself. These questions, and your answers, will clarify the issue and help you make better decisions. So, in effect, we provide phrases and questions to use with others, and phrases and questions to ask yourself to help you make decisions that will profit you and your business.

Invitation to Our Small Business Web Site

It's simply impossible to cover every aspect of owning and operating a small business in a book this size. We've created a Web site for those interested in small business, and more specifically, for you, the reader of this book. It's called the Free Small Business Resource Center, and you can find links to hundreds of excellent expert articles on all aspects of small business, special offers of interest to small business, and our small business blog where you can interact with us. Our address is **http://smallbusiness411.org**, and we hope to see you there.

Acknowledgments

We would like to acknowledge the help and assistance of John Woods and Robert Magnan, who made this book possible. Both have been an integral part in the development of all of my books. We'd also like to thank the folks at McGraw-Hill who continue to be supportive, and their editors who catch the glitches in the writing.

Dedication

This book is dedicated to our parents, Pat and SV, and Isabelle and Peter.

About the Authors

Robert Bacal is the CEO and founder of Bacal & Associates, a small business focusing on management and business consulting, publishing, and promoting learning in the workplace. His business was founded in 1992. This is Robert's seventh business book published by McGraw-Hill, in addition to several books with other publishers. Robert invites you to visit the Free Small Business Resource Center at **http://smallbusiness411.org** where you will find his small business blog and numerous free resources for small business. Robert is available for conferences and keynotes on various business and interpersonal topics.

Nancy Moore has been an integral part of the growth and success of Bacal & Associates, contributing to the development of the company's Web sites, editing and contributing to previous books, and helping with business strategy. Previously, Nancy worked as a systems analyst in the financial sector.

Both Robert and Nancy were born in Montreal, Quebec, and currently live near Ottawa, Ontario, Canada.

Chapter 1
Introduction

Some people gush glowingly about the joys of owning or running a small business. The sense of freedom, the joys of succeeding on your own, the financial returns, and the "no more idiot bosses" are often the things that both attract and reward successful business owners—or at least that's the dream. There's a dark flip side, though.

For every happy, successful small business owner, there is someone else who has encountered grief, financial ruin, family conflict, and even divorce. Not everyone is cut out to start or run a small business, because it's hard. It's really hard. It's challenging, and it requires behavioral skills (what you do), linguistic skills (how you communicate), and cognitive skills (how you think) that not everyone possesses.

This book is intended to help you plan, think about, and develop your business—and succeed. At minimum, you will find out whether you are suited for the small business life. There's more value here than that, though. You will learn what you need to know to succeed, both financially and personally. The book is relevant not only to new business owners, though. The skills, thinking, and behaviors needed to start a business are pretty much the same ones as needed to manage a small business, even an old established one. So if you are thinking about starting a small business or buying into one, if you already own one, or if you are responsible for running a small business for someone else, this book is for you.

Good News About Small Business Failures

Let's start with some encouraging news about small business.

If you've researched the small business world, you've probably come across some rather disturbing numbers about the failure rates of small business, particularly during the first year or two. There are numbers that indicate the failure rate is as high as 90 percent of new businesses. Others indicate the number is somewhere between 60 and 70 percent. There are also some figures that are at least a little more optimistic. That doesn't sound promising, does it?

There are several things you need to know about these numbers before you let them depress or discourage you.

First, it is probably accurate to say that we don't really know, with certainty, what the small business failure rate actually is. The studies use so many different criteria for "failure" that the results are hard to interpret. For example, some studies classify as failures small businesses that have been sold. However, in this era, starting a business with a clear "exit" strategy is a common and lucrative practice. Ask the Web entrepreneurs who were bought out by giants for millions. Failures? Hardly! So, number one—the statistics, best called *estimates*, regarding business failures are all over the block.

Second, the rates of failure are quite different for different industries and types of business and from region to region. Overall failure rates simply do not help you determine the chances of success for *your* business in *your field* and in *your geographic location*.

The bottom line about small business failures is this: A fair number of small businesses fail. We don't know exactly what that number is. Even if we did know the overall number, it wouldn't be useful, because it wouldn't tell us what *your* chances are. Your ability to succeed has little to do with the "odds," but almost everything to do with your skills, resources, and, above all, the decisions you make, even before you open your doors.

More Small Business Good News for the 2000s

It's arguably the best time in the history of humanity to start or run a small business. Why? The answer is simple. Technology has increased your options exponentially and has magnified the capabilities of any businessperson, in terms of business functions. Take a look at the following smattering of business tasks and activities:

- Answering telephone calls
- Designing sales brochures
- Reproducing paperwork
- Sending paperwork to clients
- Collaborating with clients or partners/employees
- Renting and managing office space
- Reaching large numbers of potential clients or customers
- Tracking business functions (accounting, sales, employees)
- Publishing a book

In 1967 these business activities took time, personnel, or a level of expertise that most small business owners might lack. Everything happened more slowly, too.

Now we have faxes and e-mails. We have the capability to run a business without the expenses of operating a physical office or store, if we choose. We can reach a large number of potential clients without spending millions on advertising, at least theoretically. We no longer need to be tied to our office phones or employ someone to answer the phone. Small business owners can use out-of-the-box accounting packages to do the basics of managing their businesses. Do you want to market to England, but your business is in Hoboken, New Jersey? Not a problem. Use the Internet. Selling globally has never been easier or cheaper.

We can even hold meetings with people located all over the world, using computer video and audio, without boarding an airplane—or even changing out of our pajamas. And on and on. Many small businesses simply couldn't have existed even a few decades ago.

More options exist now, not only for business functions, but also for the kind of business you might develop. New technologies have created new industries where small business structures can excel. For example, you can be a Web site developer, a search engine consultant, a writer for the Internet—work that did not exist 20 years ago.

There's simply more freedom and more possibilities. It's also, in an odd way, more complicated than ever before. Which brings us to the "bad news," or perhaps we should call it the "reality" of small business.

The Bad News? Heavy Dose of Reality

As with many things in life, the good news about small business needs to be tempered by the other side of "the double-edged sword." While it's true that small business owners can leverage technology to do things impossible 20 years ago and that technology has provided more options and lowered barriers to entry into small business, it brings new challenges.

That same technology that lowers the entry barriers for you has also lowered the entrance barriers for everyone else. That means, at least generally, more competition in many sectors. It's true that not all the competition will be a threat to well-run businesses, since many of the competitors are not serious or competent, but it's still a consideration. For example, if you started an Internet-based business in 1998, your chances of success would have been higher than in 2008, simply because there was generally less competition in 1998. As another example, with the advent of Internet-based retailers like Amazon.com, the competition for consumer dollars has shifted, making it much more difficult to run certain types of business that would compete in Amazon's marketplace. Now if you want to own a small bookstore, not only must you compete in price and selection with the local brick-and-mortar giants, but you must also compete with online companies that seem to have infinite resources.

The bottom line: competition arises out of the ease associated with starting a business, but different sectors and types of businesses are impacted differentially. There are a huge number of small businesses that are run terribly, though, so the increased competition may not be as critical as one would think. Once again, the decisions you make about your small business are going to determine the degree to which you are affected by increased competition.

Another reality of our society has an impact on the small business environment. The world is a very complex place, and it's more complex in a number of ways. For example, in starting a retail business or a restaurant, the requirements and issues involved—such as government regulations, inspections, legalities, supplier relationships—were much simpler going back three or four decades. There are more things to consider and more rules and regulations now. That means things go more slowly; and often in business, particularly at the start-up stage, delay means money.

Complexity also means the decisions you make are more critical and important and they require expert, specialized, and readily available knowledge and skills. The knowledge and skills necessary for doing business now are much greater than ever. You need to know more. You need to have people to help you who have expertise in areas in which you do not have enough.

What does all of this mean for you? Starting or running a small business can bring a great deal of joy and a sense of accomplishment. However, to get the rewards, whether financial or personal, you need to face a multitude of challenges, in terms of managing both the business and yourself. You need to know a lot. You need to have a lot of skills. You need to manage yourself and your personal life so that part of your world is in balance with the requirements of running your business, or you burn yourself out and you burn out your family and social relationships.

Effective Decision Making, Effective Small Businesses

What makes a small business successful? If you look at the research, you'll find what you'd expect. Successful small businesses tend to be well managed, provide a good product or service, maintain a reliable and predictable cash flow, be well planned, be marketed well, and so on.

When you take a closer look and talk with successful business owners, you can find out more. First and foremost, there isn't *one* way to succeed in small business. One owner does well because she's a great marketer. Another succeeds because he's a genius in creating services and products with high profit margins. Another is simply phenomenal at customer service. Yet another achieves success primarily because he hires great, motivated employees.

You'll find that most successful business owners have a variety of strengths, but they always have weaknesses too, since it's impossible to be expert and effective at all aspects of business. That's all pretty good news, because it means you don't have to be perfect to succeed. It also means that, ultimately, you have to use your strengths effectively and minimize your weaknesses.

How do you do that? You make good decisions. In fact, it may be that the single most important determinant of small business success is effective decision making. Make the right decisions, and you prosper. Make bad ones, and your business suffers. Make really, really bad ones, and you file for bankruptcy!

Mind you, it's much easier to say "Make good decisions" than it is to actually make good decisions. Here's why. Most of the decisions made in business, or at least the really important ones, are made in a very ambiguous, complex world, where the proper path is unclear. For almost every decision you make in business, you'll be able to imagine or foresee positives and negatives. Each decision is going to come with some unknown consequences that you cannot necessarily anticipate because you can't see into the future.

You can only do your best in making decisions. Pay attention to all the factors and the possible consequences, think them through, and ask the right questions. Then you act on your decisions.

That brings us to this book. You'd think that, from the title, the book is about what you say to people—"Perfect Phrases." Well, yes and no. What you say to people is important in determining your successes and failures. Say the wrong thing to the bank's loan officer, and you may lose financing. Negotiate badly with a supplier, and you might lose an important deal. Phrase things badly with customers, and you can watch their backs as they walk out the door.

In this book, though, we look at phrases as the stuff of thought and the stuff of effective decision making. What you say to yourself (how you think) and the questions you ask and the answers you give *will* determine how effective your business decisions will be. If you ask the wrong questions, you'll simply make wrong decisions. Make the wrong decisions, and you're done; your business is gone.

Using This Book

We've tried to structure this book in a way that roughly follows the chronology of choosing and starting a business; so, for example, we've put early on in the book topics like planning and assessing whether small business is for you.

Introduction

If you're rather new to small business, we suggest you actually start at the beginning and at least glance at each chapter. Doing so will familiarize you with the issues and challenges of creating and managing a small business. If you're a new business owner or manager, you can consult this book.

If you're more experienced in small business, you may want to use this book just as needed, once you've familiarized yourself with the content. If you encounter an issue, you'll probably find it addressed in this book; check the contents to quickly find what you need. However, if you use this book only "as needed," you may miss out on learning about things you haven't considered. And one way in which this book can contribute to helping your small business succeed is by alerting you to issues, challenges, and solutions that you simply hadn't thought about. Each chapter concludes with a few brief guiding principles to which you should pay special attention.

Consider using this book and its content as a basis for talking with other people. Nobody can think of everything. Nobody can make perfect decisions every time. It's almost always wise to get input from other people, and you can use this book as a basis to do so. For example, have your spouse or other family members look at the chapters on work-life balance with you and talk about how your family can help to make it work. Or use the book to identify some key questions you'd like to ask another business owner and then go ask.

We also invite you to visit our small business support Web site at **smallbusiness411.org**, where you will find an extensive library of helpful small business articles, advice, and an opportunity to interact with us.

Chapter 2
Beginning—Entrepreneurs, Start Your Thinking

So much of the fate of a small business has to do with how well the people making the decisions plan their strategy and tactics and how good their decisions are. The decisions to be made when starting out are critical. Make the right decisions, and you lay a foundation for long-term success. Make the wrong ones, and you will end up with a small business that is "nasty, brutish, and short," as philosopher Thomas Hobbes characterized the natural state of human beings.

To make the right decisions, you have to ask the right questions of yourself and of others. That's what we'll look at in this chapter.

Deciding if Business Ownership/ Management Is for You

Your personal characteristics—your values, attitudes, goals, skills, and knowledge—will determine whether you are suited to own or run a small business. Here are some questions you need to ask yourself. Consider asking other people who know you for their perspectives on the questions. This will provide a more balanced, objective perception of your "business self."

- Can you tolerate extreme uncertainty and ambiguity?
- How comfortable are you with living in financial insecurity?
- Do you enjoy competition?
- Do you have enough self-discipline to create your own schedules and abide by them?
- Are you willing to seek out expert help and listen to it?
- Can you adapt your thinking quickly and comfortably?
- Are you typically high energy?
- Are you willing and able to put in long hours into a business—many more hours each day than you would in a salaried position?
- Are you comfortable with the fact that your business and responsibility for it may be on your mind 24/7?
- Do you have the physical stamina to undertake the responsibilities, particularly in the first years?
- Do you thrive on stress?
- Are you able to detach from stressful situations and to rest and recover?

- Are you prepared to spend less "free" time with your family?
- Are you prepared to reduce some of your favorite leisure activities when work pressures intrude (which they often do)?
- Are you typically self-motivated?
- Do you enjoy multitasking, and are you good at it?
- Do you enjoy being attentive to detail while keeping an eye on the "big picture"?
- Do you tolerate interruption well?
- Can you be extremely organized and focused when required?
- Do you have a *realistic* idea of what running a small business involves?
- Are you good at maintaining a balance between work activities and other, necessary healthy activities (such as recreation and exercise)?

Start-up Knowledge and Skills

Your knowledge, skills, strengths, and weaknesses are going to dictate the kind of business you will succeed with, your preferences for type of business, and your willingness and ability to seek out help from others to compensate for any lack of expertise. The questions here will help you start a self-assessment process.

- What strengths do you have that apply to almost any business?
- What strengths do you have that apply to only certain types of business?
- What weaknesses do you have that may interfere with general business success?
- What weaknesses do you have that might cause you to rule out specific business types?
- How can you remedy any weaknesses by getting help from others or by developing your skills?
- What business-related skills do you really want to apply because it's very satisfying to you to use them?
- What special business-specific skills or knowledge do you possess that will provide a competitive advantage?
- How can you leverage your uniqueness to provide a competitive advantage?

Advice and Input: The Help of Strangers?

It's nice to think a person can succeed in small business as a loner, handling everything without help. That thought may be nice, but it's an unrealistic and exceedingly destructive fantasy. Here's where we'll look at the availability of substantive (nonemotional) support from others.

- Do you have connections and a network in the field or business area that you're choosing?
- Are there friends and/or other people with established expertise whom you can trust to give you honest feedback and guidance about your plans and business management?
- Have you explored or when will you explore organizations in your area that may provide assistance to small business (e.g., Small Business Administration or Canada Business, local or state government, SCORE in the United States, banks)?
- Have you identified an accountant with experience in the types of businesses you're interested in, so that you can consult him or her before committing to a particular small business path?
- Have you identified a lawyer with experience in the types of businesses you're interested in, so you can consult him or her before committing to a particular small business path?
- Are you comfortable with and do you trust the professional help you will need to retain for your small business?
- Have you explored university or college programs that might offer free or low-cost business advice or the services of an intern?
- Do your family members understand and support your decision to start a business?

Social and Family Support

Since entrepreneurs tend to be results-oriented, it's often the case that they neglect social and family issues and their needs for social and family supports. Eventually, isolation, workaholism, and family problems, if neglected, can destroy the business. So the question here is the degree to which you have the support of family members and friends and whether they can provide emotional support and life balance.

- With whom can you blow off steam about the challenges of small business? Who will have some understanding and empathy?

- What people can you count on to help you keep some balance between social and work aspects of your life and with whom you can spend time?

- Whom can you trust to look at your business actions honestly and critically with you and to help you to correct mistakes?

- Do your friends understand you may be less available to them once you're running your business?

- Do you have any friends who have flexible schedules so you can meet with them?

- Do you have friends who will encourage you to keep perspective and balance your life between work and healthy other pursuits?

- Are there organizations you can join where you can meet people encountering similar challenges and where you can make friends?

- Is your immediate family likely to be supportive even if it requires financial restraint for a while?

Financial Resources

The financial resources you have available are going to affect almost every aspect of your business, including the kinds of businesses possible and the path you take from start-up to stability. Here are a few questions to consider.

- If you earn absolutely nothing in your first complete year of business, can you (and your family) survive without intolerable hardship?
- What level of financial risk can you (and your family) assume for the first two years?
- Do you have some sort of safety net if the business fails?
- Will you require funds from a bank or other sources? Who? How much?
- Where will you find financial investors (if necessary)?
- Is your credit rating high enough to allow for obtaining business loans in the future, even if you don't foresee the need right now?

Clarifying Values and Motivations

There are many reasons why people decide to enter into small business. Entrepreneurs differ significantly on their reasons, of course, because people value different things. It's essential to be self-aware enough to know what is important to you and why you want to run a small business and to assess whether your reasons are based on sound realities or on fantasies and beliefs that are not founded firmly on the realities of small business.

Here's a checklist of phrases to help you think about what's important to you. Identify which are true for you, or rank them in order of importance. Then think about whether owning a small business will move you closer to your values and motivations or farther away. (Several of these phrases express motivations that tend to be based on unrealistic expectations or beliefs.)

- I want to make money fast.
- I want to be independent and make my own decisions.
- I'd like to work shorter hours.
- I'm tired of being pushed and pulled by things beyond my control.
- I believe I can make more money than by working for someone else.
- I have talents I can't use if I'm working for someone else.
- I value the creativity and variety of owning my own business.
- I want to create a product or service people will love.
- I want to make a living while helping people in need.

- I want to have more time to learn and apply new things.
- I want to create something I can pass on to my children.
- I love and want the challenge.
- I want to spend more time doing things I'm passionate about.
- I want to do things I love.
- I want the opportunity to lead and manage employees.
- I want more freedom and flexibility in my life.
- I'm looking to create long-term stability in my life.
- I'm excited about building a large, growing business over the years.
- I can't find a regular job that makes use of my abilities.

Defining Success

Running a small business can be like running on an perpetual treadmill unless you have some idea of what constitutes success for you and your business. Having an idea of your goals for success can also help guide you in making decisions. As you can see below, you can define success in various ways—wealth and/or financial security, recognition and status, freedom of action, leisure time.

- In two years, I'd like to be able to reduce my time spent on the business to 20 hours a week.
- I'd feel successful if I'm still in business five years from now.
- I'd consider my business successful if I can take a salary of $100,000 a year.
- Success would be taking a 20 percent market share within five years.
- I'd deem the business successful when I could sell it for $1 million—that's my exit strategy.
- Success would mean being able to attract independent investors within five years.
- If I can develop a strong reputation of expertise and respect for my abilities and skills, I'd consider that part of my business success.
- I want to make enough money to live a modest lifestyle while working at something that is my passion.
- Success would mean being able to give back to my community in the form of helping children at risk.
- Success would mean knowing I made a positive difference in at least one person's life.

- Success would mean being able to create well-paying jobs within my community.
- Success would mean the ability to sponsor community events and charities.
- Success would mean becoming franchised across North America.
- Success means paying for my children's undergraduate and graduate studies.

Involving Family, Trusted Advisors

Due to the financial, mental, and time demands of starting and running a small business, family and friends can either help or hinder you. Perhaps more important, starting and running a business can cause stress for the people close to you and your relationships with them. Here are some perfect phrases to use to explore these issues with family members and friends.

The following are questions to ask yourself.

- Am I attentive, rather than dismissive, when family/friends offer solicited feedback?
- Can I engage in conversations with family members about issues other than my business?
- Do I let last-minute business issues interfere with my family plans or obligations consistently?
- Am I up-to-date on the lives of my family members and their individual challenges?
- Am I making and meeting enough family commitments?
- Am I still remembering and acknowledging dates special to family members, such as birthdays and anniversaries?

Here are some phrases you can use to open dialog with family, friends, and trusted advisors.

- Are we discussing and reviewing our expectations and relationship issues often enough?
- I'd like to make sure you (family) understand that we might have to give up a few things for a year or two.
- I'm hoping you'll feel comfortable reining me in if my ideas get too unrealistic.

- The best thing you can do is offer suggestions if you think I'm going off in the wrong direction.
- You know I tend to be disorganized, so I would greatly appreciate anything you can do to help organize things around here.
- When I'm working in my office (home), we need to all be a little quieter and not interrupt.
- Since things are going to be so busy, let's make sure we all eat together every day and spend some good time together.

Guiding Principles

Asking the right questions, from square one, is critical to the success of any small business, since it leads to making the right decisions. When your values, goals, and motivations are all aligned, you are more likely to succeed. Determine the degree to which a small business will fulfill your needs and wants. Make sure you are not basing your decisions on unrealistic fantasies about small business. From the beginning, evaluate, appreciate, and grow your financial, social, familial, and other support networks.

Chapter 3
Your Formal Business Plan

Once you have defined your business, know what you want to do, and have assessed your suitability, the next step is to prepare a formal business plan. In short, a business plan outlines where you want to go, how you are going to get there, barriers you might encounter, financial expectations and projections, your market niche, and some other essential factors.

A formal business plan is slightly different from an informal one, in that the formal version is developed and polished for others to read and evaluate. For example, a banker will expect a formal plan before even considering a business loan application. An informal plan is less rigorous and can be less polished, since its function is to help guide you. If you do not need to impress or convince anybody or to obtain any capital or support, then an informal business plan may work for you. However, a formal plan, since it requires more effort, forces you to think about your business in a disciplined way. Also, if you do one, you'll have it on hand, just in case. You might also want to write slightly different plans for different purposes.

The business plan will:

- Encourage you to think in depth about your business, its strengths and weaknesses, the financial requirements and risks, and so on, helping you to prepare to overcome barriers
- Demonstrate to investors and bankers (or other parties) that you have done sufficient and appropriate research
- Help inform others about your business
- Push you to forecast critical parts of your business in financial terms, including projected revenues and start-up costs

On these pages are the components of a business plan and examples of phrases that you can customize to use in your plan.

Executive Summary

The executive summary provides an overview of the key points in the business plan. A business plan may range from 15 to 200-plus pages; the summary represents the "business at a glance." Normally it includes a sentence or two from each major section of the plan document. Only the most relevant and important details should be presented in the executive summary. It should provide enough information to interest the reader in reading the rest of the plan.

Here are a few questions to help guide you in writing your executive summary.

- Who will be the most important people reading the plan?
- What will be their main concerns?
- What information will they want most?
- What information can I put in the summary to both grab interest and give needed answers quickly?

Business Overview

In the business overview section of your business plan, you want to provide enough information so the reader understands where your business is right now, where it has been, and where it is going in the future. Here are some examples of perfect phrases for the subcategories in this section—business description; business history; and ownership, management, and staffing.

BUSINESS DESCRIPTION

This description should capture the essence of your business in a brief statement.

- Bob's Landscaping will provide economical gardening services to commercial and residential customers in Yonkers, Mount Vernon, Bronxville, and Tuckahoe.
- Bob's Yangtze Restaurant is and will remain the primary eat-in and takeout restaurant specializing in Northern Chinese Dishes in the Yonkers region.
- Pizza Bon is a franchise outlet of the Pizza Bon chain, operating with exclusive territorial rights in the area bounded by the Saw Mill Parkway, Executive Boulevard, the Hudson River, and the Bronx.
- Business Unlimited will provide consulting and training services to small business owners looking to expand their revenues through franchising opportunities.

BUSINESS HISTORY

Here you tell where you've been with the business, if it's not new. Include what would be relevant to the people whom you want to reach with your strategic plan.

- Pizza Bon has been in operation since 1992.
- It's been in its present location since 2001.
- Strategic Solutions Consulting expanded from three employees to six employees in 2006.
- Strategic Solutions Consulting was purchased from the previous owner in 2002.
- The business was registered in 1998 but did not start actively trading until 2001 to provide an opportunity to build operating capital.

OWNERSHIP, MANAGEMENT, AND STAFFING

Readers will want to know who owns the company and how it is owned (corporation, sole proprietor, general partnership, limited partnership, limited liability company), and they will want to understand who is responsible for managing critical business functions (board of directors, CEO, financial officers). This is particularly true for those who may be investing in your company, since they will want to be confident about the management team. For that reason, you may want to include basic biographical information in this section to the extent it helps build confidence.

- Pizza Bon is solely owned and operated by Bonnie Albert, with management support from the Pizza Bon franchising staff. [Short bio of owner could go here.]
- Business Unlimited is operated as a joint equal partnership between Aubrey Smith and Helen Arnnott. Helen, the managing partner, has 10 years' experience in ....
- Strategic Solutions is operated as a limited liability company with three members: ....

- Our board of directors is currently composed of the following five people: ....
- The CEO is Mabel Smith, who was previously COO of Sugarblogs Inc.
- Business Unlimited has five full-time employees involved in direct delivery of consulting services to customers.
- There are three sales representatives on staff with a total of 60 years of sales experience in the field, in addition to two administrative employees offering support to staff.

Vision and Mission Statements

Vision and mission statements are defined in various ways, but there's no need to get caught up on definitions. Think of your vision statement as your "dream" about where you want the company to end up, and think of your mission statement as its overall purpose. You can combine them for the sake of your strategic plan, as follows.

- We want to be known as the best pizza parlor in Muskogee.
- We intend to make our name synonymous with high-quality, best-of-class widgets.
- We see ourselves as the primary distributor of self-help audio products in the world.
- We want to be a driving force in the development of the market for widgets, by developing new widget products.
- By being the most innovative company in our sector, we plan on becoming a dominant player in the market in our geographic region.

Key Objectives, Goals, and Initiatives

Your vision and mission tend to be general. Objectives, goals, and initiatives tell the reader, in more specific terms, how you are going to become what you wish to become. In this section describe your financial and market share goals, plus any specific initiatives that are important. While your vision can be oriented toward dreams and your mission can be idealistic, your key objectives should be realistic goals you believe you will achieve.

- Within the first two years, obtain a 5 percent market share in our field within the geographic region of ....
- Reach the $100,000 mark for gross sales by January 1, 2010.
- Become profitable by January 1, 2010.
- Increase distribution into major retail chains by 25 percent within three years.
- Lease or obtain an option on additional adjacent space to allow facilities expansion in 2010.
- Deliver 50 public seminars in year one, escalating to 100 in year two.
- Develop five new product lines within the first three years to support our initial products and provide up-sell options.

Products, Services, and Market

In this major section you explain what you will produce and/or what you will sell, and you provide information about the market and your marketing strategies—past, present, and future. Give details and be specific. While you don't want to talk down to people who will be reading your business plan, you can't assume that they will be familiar with your area of business.

DESCRIPTION OF PRODUCTS AND SERVICES

Describe your products and services here. Provide enough information for readers unfamiliar with your type of business to understand the value of what you can offer. If appropriate, include future products or services as well as what you offer currently, being careful to distinguish between what you provide at present and what products or services are in development. It's also important to indicate the legal ownership and status of products and patents related to the products.

- Lock-picking devices are used by law enforcement and registered locksmiths.
- We produce a line of lock-picking devices made of stainless steel that can be used for both automotive and home emergency situations.
- We provide management consulting services to the top manufacturing companies in central Ohio, enabling them to streamline their manufacturing process.
- We make and deliver a wide range of designer pizzas to the area surrounding Fenway Park.

- Our lock-picking tools are patented by Yutakeum Limited and produced under exclusive license by our company.
- We design solid-state memory-based MP3 players that are both innovative and inexpensive and license them to manufacturers around the world.
- Our MP3 players are protected by worldwide patents. [Insert numbers and other details here.]
- Our legal services will focus on meeting the needs of corporations incorporated in the state of Delaware.
- Products will be distributed through our existing national distribution agreements with Hume-Gray Hardware and Wellie-Mart at over 700 retail outlets.

MARKET

Your products or services may be great, but if nobody wants to buy what you're offering, you'll fail. In this section, outline your target customers, key features and competitive advantages, and your marketing direction and opportunities.

You can start by describing the size and demographics of the market, adding any other pertinent information (such as whether it's underserved in your area).

- According to recent statistics compiled by the Boston Chamber of Commerce, 60 percent of small businesses plan on hiring a management consultant in the next five years. (small business consultant)
- Our prime demographic—18- to 25-year-old males—buys an average of 2.6 takeout pizzas each month. (pizza restaurant)
- Sidewalk traffic past our intended location exceeds 1,000 people per hour. (discount retail store)

- There are 20,000 homes in our business area, and, on average, each home orders takeout food at least once a week. (pizza restaurant)
- Each year, 40 percent of small businesses in the state hire outside firms to assist them with human resource issues. (small business consultant)
- Online advertising is projected to increase by 10 percent each year for the next three years. (ad-supported online business)

Next, cite the key features or competitive advantages of the products or services you'll be offering. For almost every product or service you can imagine, there will be competitors that are in your area or that can service your area. You need to explain, to both yourself and your readers, how what you will be offering is better, faster, stronger, etc. In short, tell what separates your products and services from what competitors offer. Outline your competitive advantages.

- Unlike other management consulting firms, we offer one-stop solutions.
- We provide firm quotes to customers so they always know exactly what their product/service will cost, while other firms quote soft numbers or charge by the hour.
- We own our own production facilities, so we can control our production costs better than competitors, thus offering lower retail costs and/or higher profit margins.
- We have one of the best locations in the city for delivery pizza.
- Competitors license the rights to similar product lines at considerable extra cost, while we actually own the patents and do not pay royalties.

- Our Web site, which will generate significant sales, has been up for five years and has an established visitor base, unlike the sites of our competitors.
- Strategic pricing places our prices at 5 percent below the average price in the marketplace.

The next part of the market section is marketing directions and opportunities. State briefly how you will reach your target market and how you will create and maximize marketing opportunities.

- Product endorsements have been secured from prominent experts and will be featured in our print and online promotional materials and in media ads.
- Sales generated by our Web site marketing exceed $200,000 a year, a figure we expect to double in 2010 with only minimal additional marketing costs.
- Our marketing budget for the first year will be $10,000, allocated primarily to building our Internet presence and brand awareness.
- Second-year marketing will focus on taking advantage of media contacts in our industry, arranging for feature stories in the print media, and presenting at trade shows.
- CEO F. Kruger continues to do pro bono presentations and seminars, both locally and nationally, to increase brand and product awareness.
- Strategic marketing agreements are in place with several complementary companies to facilitate cross-marketing and cross-referrals.

Implementation Plan

The people who will be reading your business plan will want to feel confident that you know what you will need to do to achieve your business and financial goals and objectives. They want to know not only what you plan on doing, but also when, particularly if they are investing in you. Obviously you can't include every detail for the next 10 years, but you need to include enough to show you are competent and have the bases covered. Here are a few examples.

- Procure appropriate licenses and zoning variances by March 2010.
- Complete international patent applications to secure trade and service marks.
- Extend current office premises leases to provide long-term stability.
- Double distribution channel reach by concluding distribution deals with Kruger Enterprises.
- Retain outsourced HR support to help with hiring of new staff members by April 2011.
- Hire one new consultant and two new salespeople by June 2011.

Financial Plans

Readers of your formal business plan are going to pay special attention to the financial details. While you phrase some sections of your business plan in generalities (although specifics are almost always better), financial plans require a considerable amount of detail. This can be a challenge when you are providing projections and need to produce specific numbers that are best guesses.

Particularly, readers want to know where you will get your start-up money, what your expenses will be (start-up and ongoing), how much profit you expect, how much you will gross in sales, and, if they are investing, how long it will take for them to receive a good return on their investment. They also want enough information to assess the financial risks associated with the business.

If you are not familiar with accounting practices (and if you aren't an accountant, you are not familiar enough), we strongly advise that you obtain the help of an accountant conversant with standard accounting practices used in your industry and/or required by law. There are standard, expected ways to state financials, and it's important that you abide by them to protect yourself legally.

Your financial planning section will include both explanations and text plus summaries in the form of appropriate tables and graphs. Pay special attention to the tables and graphs, because readers are going to look for certain numbers in the tables, rather than read the text. For example, balance sheets (past, present, and/or projected) are critical. You cannot replace these tables and charts with text.

Here are some subcategories you'll probably want to include in the financial section.

FINANCIAL OVERVIEW

This section provides the equivalent of an executive summary with respect to profits, losses, and projections. It should contain enough basic information for the reader to get a sense of profitability, sales levels, margins, and so on. If they want additional detail, they can look at subsequent sections.

- Net profitability will be reached in our second full year of business.
- First-year sales are projected to be $180,000, doubling to $360,000 in year two.
- Capital investment requirements in the first two years will reach $50,000.
- Net profit after taxes will be $80,000 in year one, which is 12 percent of anticipated gross sales.
- Operating expenses are projected at 2 percent of gross sales.
- Debt load for the first two years is approximately $200,000, repayable at 12 percent interest.
- Total start-up capital required is $300,000, with $100,000 supplied by the owner and the remainder by private investors.
- Start-up capital will be used to renovate our manufacturing equipment.

BUSINESS ASSUMPTIONS

A business plan looks to the future and outlines what is

expected financially from the business, in terms of expenses, capital investments, sales, revenues, and profit margins. Because it's future-oriented, the numbers are projections. Projections are based on certain assumptions about the industry, economy, and business. Readers need to know what assumptions you are making that underlie your projected numbers. State these assumptions with considerable care and attention, since readers will lose confidence in your plan if your assumptions are unrealistic. Consider providing rationales for your assumptions, and be prepared to defend them.

- Projected sales are based on an average 8 percent increase in gross sales per annum across the industry.
- Commission estimates/sales are based on a real estate market with average selling prices growing at 10 percent per year.
- Overall revenue is based on an increased demand for fuel-efficient vehicles and increased gasoline costs.
- Net profits are projected on the basis of an average 30 percent vacancy rate.
- We anticipate sales to continue to increase as in the last five years, at a rate of 15 percent per year.
- We expect to reach 20 percent total market share in 2010, based on our past two years of growth.
- Projections are based on completion of distribution deals with at least two major distributors within the first year.

CASH FLOW

Readers of your plan want to know that your business is sustainable, in both the short term (month to month) and longer term (year to year). This section provides historical, current, and projected information regarding revenues and expenses. Cash flows—past, present, or future—are best represented in charts and figures, accompanied by text to summarize.

- In 2008, a positive monthly cash flow was achieved for every month.
- Based on our historical numbers, we anticipate positive cash flows every month, except for January, when our sales are slowest.
- Due to major expenditures required in our first three months of business, we anticipate a negative cash flow in the first three months.
- Projected cash flows for the first three years will be sufficient to retire all outstanding company debt.

COSTS AND FINANCIAL REQUIREMENTS

Normally, you would include tables, graphs, and other figures to outline the various costs of your business and incorporate any capital requirements. Again, the purpose here is to provide enough information so that readers understand that you know what you are doing and that your business is based on sound assumptions and financial projections.

You would most likely include three tables: for cost of goods, for capital expenditures and/or requirements, and for overhead/costs. Following are some of the things that you might put in a summary associated with each table and within each table. Keep your summaries short, since numbers are best presented and understood in tabular format.

Costs of Goods

- Average unit cost for our widgets is 22.3 cents.
- 23 percent of the cost of each widget is for raw materials, 57 percent is for labor costs, and other overhead (administrative costs) constitutes 20 percent of the total cost.
- We anticipate a 15 percent decrease in per-unit production cost as a result of increased volume production.
- Customer acquisition costs will be around $8.00 per purchasing customer.

Capital Expenditures and/or Requirements

- Initial capital investment in year one is $150,000.
- 30 percent of initial first-year capital investment is allocated to develop the technical infrastructure to service customers (computers, communications equipment).
- Yearly capital investment of $200,000 is expected to purchase production/manufacturing equipment to expand production by 30 percent in each year for the next five years.
- As a service-based consulting business, initial capital investments will be minimal, less than $15,000.

Overhead/Costs

- Total operating expenses for year one are projected at $200,000. This figure includes start-up costs, hiring, rental of premises, marketing costs, and … [insert other items].
- In year one marketing costs will constitute 60 percent of operating expenses, dropping to 30 percent of operating expenses in year two and year three.

Guiding Principles

Your business plan must be based on reality, not on wishful thinking, or it will lead you in the direction of failure. Unrealistic assumptions and numbers will lead others to conclude that you are not believable and therefore a bad risk. Projections should be realistic and supported by evidence.

Where possible, use specifics rather than generalizations.

Incorporate contingency analyses in your plan to anticipate unforeseen or negative circumstances and events (such as sales 14 percent lower than expected). Think about what you will do when things go wrong. Convince readers you've covered the bases.

Writing a business plan is an art as well as a science. There are many ways to do it that can work well. If you need the best business plan you can develop (for example, to get a bank loan), consider getting help from someone who's done some business plans.

Before you show your plan to important readers, get it reviewed by as many disinterested parties as possible. Ask them to look at the writing, particularly in terms of how credible you sound and how realistic it is. Ask them to be picky about flaws. At this stage you need to know what's wrong and not what's right. Family members are not the best reviewers, since they will tend to be either overly harsh or afraid of hurting your feelings.

Chapter 4
Presenting Your Business Plan or Business Proposal

There are times when your business plan or business proposal has to stand on its own as a document. It must convey information in writing in such a way as to ensure a clear understanding of your business and show that you are competent to make your business succeed.

There are also times when you will be asked to present your business plan or proposal to one person or a group of people. For example, your bank may ask you to do a brief oral presentation on your business plan to a loan officer or to the lending committee. Or you may need to explain a business proposal to the board of directors of another firm.

Most business presentations must do the following:

- Convey information (usually quickly and succinctly).
- Make you appear competent and credible to the audience.
- Convince the audience to take some form of action beneficial to you.

There are a few things to keep in mind when planning and delivering business presentations. First, the audience will usually not have read the paper version of your plan or proposal, so you must provide clear explanations that stand alone. Second, you must convey a sense of opportunity and urgency so your audience wants to become involved. Third, you must respond competently to questions from group members. Finally, keep in mind that while there are some similarities between presenting a business plan or proposal and doing a sales pitch, they are different. High-pressure tactics, wild promises, unrealistic numbers, and other less regarded sales techniques are inappropriate in presenting a plan or a proposal and are likely to ruin your credibility.

Your Goals

An effective business presentation begins with clarity of purpose. If you know what you want from your audience (your purpose), you'll be much more likely to get it. If you are unclear, it will show. Here are some statements to help you define your purpose. You can use some of these during the presentation to focus the audience, while others you may want to keep to yourself.

- I would like the loan committee to approve my business loan for $50,000.
- I'd like to be invited back to do a more detailed presentation for the CEO.
- At the end of the presentation meeting, I'd like a commitment from them to begin business negotiations.
- I want them to prepare a proposal regarding investing in my business.
- I want them to sign the contract I'm presenting to them during the meeting.
- I need a decision from the group by May 6.
- The four points I absolutely want the audience to take away at the end of the presentation are ... [list].

Audience Expectations and Needs

Know your audience. Making a business presentation involves balancing your needs with the needs and expectations of your audience. If they expect you to speak to them in a particular format, do it. If they expect a certain level of flash in your visual material, then provide it. Keep to their expectations about time limits. A common reason that business presentations fail is that the presenter ignores or violates the expectations of the group.

To meet their expectations and needs, you need to learn about them. Here are some questions to help you do so. Most of these questions involve doing research before the presentation, by either asking the contact person or otherwise finding out about the group.

- How much time can I have for the presentation?
- Who will be attending?
- What does each member of the group do, and what is his or her interest in the presentation?
- What might each person need from me in order to support my goals for the presentation and the action I want from it?
- Would this group likely expect a very slick, high-tech presentation or be more comfortable with a lower-tech, "no glitz" approach?
- How much do the group members know about the topic of my business plan or proposal?
- What are the top five points I must make with this group of people in order to succeed?

- Is there a formal leader in this group who will control the meeting or presentation?
- What is that formal leader like? What does he or she want and appreciate (e.g., brevity, details, broad overviews, specific numbers)?
- Who are the "thought leaders" in the group—the members who exert great informal influence but not necessarily any formal power?
- What might these people appreciate in a presentation?
- Is there anything else on the meeting agenda that might distract the group members from concentrating on my presentation (e.g., announcements of bad news, compelling emergency)?
- What timeline does the group have for making a decision or taking action on my plan or proposal?
- What questions is this group most likely to need answered?
- How can the individuals present contribute to the success of the plan or proposal if the group reacts as I'd like?

Preparation

There are some other things to do to prepare for your plan presentation, to make it clear, focused, organized, and dynamic. Here are some questions to consider.

- Who will take notes during the presentation (if necessary)?
- Have I rehearsed my presentation and determined how long it will probably take?
- Do I have the critical figures available in easily accessible note form, so I can refer to them if asked or if my memory falters?
- Do I have a realistic plan for arriving at the presentation site on time, with the appropriate materials and/or people and with the least possible extra stress?
- Have I checked any computers or other technology I need to use? (Check just before the presentation and multiple times.)
- Does each member of my team understand his or her role in the presentation?
- Does each team member understand when it is OK to jump into the presentation and when not to do so?
- Have I had a few people evaluate my presentation who are similar to the anticipated audience?
- Is there a meeting agenda?
- Have I organized my presentation so no single segment extends beyond six minutes?
- What is the physical space like in which I will present, and how does it affect what I can and cannot do during the presentation?

Your Introduction

Your introduction should be short. It should convey warmth, credibility, and comfort (if possible). It should explain in brief who you are, why you are there, and what action, if any, you hope your audience will take. It's also the place to indicate whether you will be accepting questions during the presentation or prefer to answer them during a special question period.

- Thank you. I'm Fred Mertz, and I'm the CEO for Mandragon Industries.

- I'm Fred Mertz, CEO of Mandragon Industries, and this is Alice Donahue, our expert on financial matters and our CFO.

- The numbers and projections I'm going to show you are based on actual numbers from the years 2000–2006.

- I'm going to explain our corporate plan and why it's worthy of your attention and investment.

- We're going to explain our business model and our revenue and profit projections. They indicate we can repay the business loan within 18 months.

- During the first 20 minutes, I'll explain the Mandragon business model. Then I'd like to answer any specific questions you may have.

- Feel free to interrupt me to ask questions as they come to mind.

- After the presentation, I hope you will be willing to begin more formal negotiations to make our partnership a reality.

Overview of the Business Plan/Proposal

Once you've introduced yourself in a paragraph or so, it's time to give an overview of what you have to offer. Here are some phrases that you can use, in addition to those included in the previous chapter on business plan content.

During the overview, you can highlight what you want from the group and begin focusing on the value proposition (selling points) from the point of view of the group members.

- Alfalfa Growers, Inc., is an established company in the agri sector looking to expand into other horse feed opportunities.
- Plynth Pizzeria has had a successful expansion of four stores in the last year and is looking for additional capital to support further expansion.
- We believe that the partnering of our two companies can help increase your market share by 10 percent, while allowing us to upgrade our manufacturing facilities to reduce production costs.
- I'm hopeful that we can come to a decision sometime this week, or we'll need to look at alternative partners.
- We hope you can make a decision on our proposal before the end of the month.
- I'm going to present some figures to support our conservative profit estimates of $100,000 in our third year.
- Your return on investment for the first three years is estimated at 12 percent per annum.

Presentation of Details

Business presentations have time limits that restrict how much detail you can provide. Balance general information with specifics. Get into details enough to show you know what you are talking about, but not so much as to put everyone to sleep. Not all details need to be presented orally, but they can be included in written materials. Take special care with financial numbers and projections so as to be specific enough while remaining realistic and not overloading the audience. Focus on the most important numbers and details.

Here are some examples. Obviously the details you should include depend on your business type, the audience, and the goals of your presentation.

- Paragon Pizza has increased its sales and its profit margins by 8 percent per annum for the last five years.
- We anticipate that by expanding using your investment capital, we can double our profits within two years.
- Based on our conservative projections, investors will recoup their investment and receive a 35 percent return in two years.
- Due to changes in the region, our target market is expanding locally by about 10 percent—or 100,000 potential customers—per year.
- Investment opportunities in our sector have outperformed similar investment opportunities in other sectors by a 15 percent per annum return on investment.
- Our patented widget is protected from simple copying, guaranteeing we will be the sole supplier for at least two years.

Use of Visuals and Handouts

The use of audiovisuals is particularly effective for business presentations. Graphics communicate complex numbers better than words. For example, a simple bar chart is a great way to show how revenue has grown over the last five years or how the market has grown over three years.

That said, presenters tend to use far too many audiovisual aids (e.g., PowerPoint or overhead slides), such that their impact is lessened. You are the main feature—any audiovisuals are there to support your presentation, not to control you. The same holds for any handouts or documents. Longer documents should be distributed after the presentation; shorter documents or information the group needs during the presentation should be provided in advance.

Here are phrases to use with your audiovisual materials.

- Let me explain what you are seeing. The blue lines represent our per-year net profit over the last five years, while the green lines represent total revenues. Both our profit margins and our net profits have increased during that time.

- Here's the architect's model of our new premises. Note the clean lines, the easy public access, and the potential for walk-by traffic.

- Here's the bottom line. (Point to the slide captioned in big letters, "Return on Investment: 55 percent in two years."

- Note the pie chart showing our historical revenue breakdown by demographic and another showing our projected revenue breakdown if we increase our marketing budgets.

- There's a copy of the graph on the screen on page 8 of your handout.

Responding to Questions and Reacting to Glitches

No matter how well you plan your presentation, things can go wrong or people can ask you challenging questions. Unexpected questions and glitches can throw you off your talk if you get flustered. On the other hand, they provide opportunities to demonstrate how calm, confident, and skillful you are. Many a business presentation outcome has been determined by how the presenter handled it when things went wrong. Here are some examples.

- That's a good question, George. I don't have those figures in my head, but if you can wait until the end of the presentation, I'll check my notes to make sure I give you exact numbers.
- (You're caught making a logical error.) You know, Jack, you are right that we didn't take that into account, so these numbers will be off by about 10 percent. I apologize, and we'll modify the planning document and get you revised copies by 5:00 this afternoon.
- Oops! Obviously the graphic isn't showing properly on the screen, so let me direct you to page 4 in your handout, and we'll work from the graphic there.
- (You notice a big coffee stain on your shirt.) And if anyone needs more coffee, let me know, since I've apparently brought some extra. (Point to your shirt—and then just ignore the stain.)
- I'm very sorry for being late. I know you are all very busy, so I'll try to stay within the time allotted.

- I want to make sure the numbers I give you are accurate, so before I continue, let's take a quick stretch break for five minutes while I consult my notes. (You can use this if you become flustered or lost.)
- Mary, I don't know the answer to your question, and I don't have those numbers in the business plan. As soon as I'm finished here, I'll call my partner and get them for you within an hour of the end of our meeting. Is that OK?

Conclusion/Summary

The conclusion of your presentation should generate energy and excitement, and it should include a reminder of the call for action or the actions you wish the audience to take as a result of your presentation. Follow the common pattern for presentations: tell them what you're going to tell them (introduction), deliver what you promised to tell them (details), and tell them what you've told them (conclusion/summary).

- I hope you share our enthusiasm about our innovative product line. I look forward to hearing from your purchasing department for your first order.
- We feel this business opportunity will continue to yield a return on your investment exceeding your current return by 50 percent.
- We hope to hear from you regarding your decision by May 5, one way or the other. After that, we'll be looking at other avenues.
- You can see that partnering in our marketing efforts will cut marketing costs for you and for us by 30 percent while increasing our marketing reach into new demographics.
- To summarize, the advantages of taking this action are clear: [reiterate advantages cited earlier]. However, there are also one or two downsides you may want to consider. [Describe them.] We believe the pluses clearly outweigh the minuses.
- There's some urgency for us to come to a decision on this, so we need your ideas by the end of the week.

- We're enthusiastic about working with you and look forward to beginning more formal negotiations about the terms of this deal.
- As soon as you let us know you are ready to go, we'll start implementing our expansion plan so we can all begin realizing the profit potential as soon as possible.

Guiding Principles

Presenting a business plan or proposal may seem similar to making a sales pitch, but it's not. There is some overlap, but you must be careful not to oversell in a presentation.

The plan or proposal document (paper handouts) and your presentation go hand in hand and need to complement each other. Both must create the same clear picture and develop a sense that you are competent and credible. Both need to be honest, easy to follow, and free of glitz and overselling. Business presentations need not be slick, expensive packages. However, the form and look of both your presentation and your business document need to meet the expectations of your readers and audience.

Keep the superlatives and exaggerations to a minimum, or even eliminate them. Trying too hard isn't convincing.

Honesty and openness are much more likely to bring about the outcomes you desire. People are good at sensing if you are trying to avoid issues or questions, dodge unpleasant news, or lack the skills to think on your feet.

The golden rule of any presentation or performance is to keep going even if things go wrong. If your equipment fails, keep going. If you lose your train of thought, take a second to gather your thoughts and keep going. Most times, don't apologize or call attention to the glitches unless you can do so in a humorous way. Your audience will appreciate it and admire you for this.

Present both positives and negatives to your proposition. A more balanced approach improves your credibility.

Chapter 5
Self-Motivation, Self-Management, and Mind-Set

The ability to motivate oneself and stay focused is absolutely essential to the success of a small business, because small business owners are responsible for so many business functions, some enjoyable and some tedious. When you're starting up, you'll probably be so motivated, you'll tend toward the obsessive, but as your business becomes stable, you may find it more and more challenging to focus and drive yourself onward.

In addition to motivation and focus, you need a mind-set that will get you through challenges and over hurdles. Every business faces bleak situations or periods of stagnation. It can feel like being stuck, as the business moves neither forward nor backward.

This chapter will help you with self-talk, affirmations, and questions you'll find useful in maintaining an appropriate level of motivation, keeping focused on your business tasks, and developing a resilient state of mind that will help you pull through tough times.

When Times Get Tough

It's a rare business that doesn't experience rough patches. Small business owners can fall prey to temporary droughts and tough times. Apart from the obvious impact on your revenue, such times play havoc with your mental attitudes, motivation levels, and confidence in your ideas and business model. Here are some phrases you can use when times get tough that will help you turn around, both business-wise and head-wise.

- I believe in my business ideas, and I know that this is only a temporary setback.
- I will use this lull to look critically at my business practices and to improve them as needed.
- This is a good time to survey my competitors to compare how they are faring in this economy.
- I need to stay current with regard to new businesses that offer the same products or services.
- I can use this opportunity to take stock of my interactions with clients and employees to ensure that I've acted with integrity in all cases.
- It's time to review my business plan to understand how I got to this point.
- I need to ensure that my market research is up-to-date.
- It is important for me to research the business trends of my products and services.
- Reviewing my market share will help me determine my next actions.
- Reviewing my financial bottom line will help me determine my plan of action.

- I need to evaluate whether we are doing things that are alienating our customers and suppliers.
- I need to consider bringing in an outside consultant so as to get a fresh mind-set in this situation.
- I need to recognize that any business has to change with time and that it's time to evaluate our present plan and update it.

Managing Your Time

Since the demands of your small business are likely to exceed the time you should make available for the tasks, time management becomes critical to the health of your business and also to your physical and mental health and your personal life. It's extremely tricky to spend enough time and yet not too much time on business tasks. It's an even bigger challenge to spend your time on the more important business functions and not on the things you enjoy doing. Here are some phrases to help you with time management.

- This is a list of tasks that I must complete today.
- This is a list of tasks to be completed by the end of the week.
- My priorities for the day are ....
- My priorities for the week are ....
- Mornings are my most productive times; therefore, I'll schedule my most difficult tasks then.
- I am not at my best in the morning; therefore, I'll try to schedule my appointments for the early afternoon.
- I will perform administrative duties (return calls, review mail, make appointments, prepare orders) at the end of my business day.
- I will keep my appointment calendar up-to-date.
- I will keep contact information for my clients, customers, and suppliers up-to-date and easily accessible.
- I will keep my company accounting system up-to-date.
- I will keep my order-and-delivery system current.
- I will keep my inventory system current.

- I will investigate client concerns within my company's stated timeline.
- I will reward myself with tasks I really enjoy doing after I've finished the tasks I need to do but dislike.
- I will delegate tasks to others when it isn't necessary to do those tasks personally.
- I will allocate my time to the tasks that I can do best or only I can do.

Creative Visualization

Part of motivation and the ability to keep going even when times are tough is to visualize success and the achievement of your business and personal goals. The better you are at imagining success in all its vivid details, the more you can use that "future state" to motivate you in the present. Of course, your success visualizations should be at least somewhat realistic since they should be achievable. Fantasies that are unattainable are not powerful motivators.

- I can see my business report showing $100,000 in net earnings and feeling like a success.
- I can picture paying cash for my late model car and enjoying my first long-distance drive with the top down, knowing I've earned the car and the vacation.
- I can feel how proud I will be to give my two employees well-deserved, year-end bonuses, and I can feel their pleasure.
- I feel honored as the audience stands up and claps for me as I receive my Entrepreneur-of-the-Year award.
- I picture myself signing copies of my book in stores and being pleased to see the many people patiently lined up to meet me.
- I can smell the freshness of the coffee in my cup as I make my way from my kitchen to my home office. I am ready to settle in for a few hours of work as I notice the family cat jumping on the office sofa settling in for a nap. "Not a bad idea," I think. "Maybe I'll stretch out, too, later."

■ I picture myself captivating an audience and feeling confident that I can help each individual sitting in front of me attain success.

■ I am sitting in my home office feeling proud of the day's progress, and I notice the beautiful weather. I am accountable to no one as I decide to take a bike ride for an hour or so. Such freedom!

■ I am excited to realize that my business is so successful that I need to hire an assistant to organize my business appointments and speaking engagements.

■ I can feel the confidence that I have upon meeting a prospective client. My handshake feels firm. I see respect when we make eye contact. I know we will do business together when the client says, "I've heard a lot of good things about you."

■ I allow myself to feel motivated to finish a long and arduous task by feeling the euphoria I will experience upon its completion.

Staying Sharp

If your success relies on making the right decisions at the right time, it's important that you do your best to remain sharp, both cognitively (your thinking) and affectively (emotionally). A stressed, tired, angry, frustrated, fearful entrepreneur makes bad decisions and is also more prone to cutting corners to relieve the discomfort. Here are some questions to help you stay on top of your game.

- Is eating a healthy breakfast part of my daily routine?
- Will listening to music (or any other audio stimulus) in the background help me to think clearly?
- Should I consider "working memory training"?
- Do I get enough sleep regularly?
- Do I get enough regular physical exercise?
- Do I drink to excess?
- Do I smoke?
- Do I take enough breaks from working?
- Do I have a healthy and moderate eating regimen?
- Am I spiritual and calm?
- Am I able to concentrate most times?
- Do I practice relaxation techniques?
- Am I aware of stress-reducing techniques?
- Do I rely on television too much to spark my creativity?
- Do I regularly read, solve puzzles, or invent what-if games to stretch my brainpower?
- Do I have an overall plan to help me keep sane, calm, and in control?
- Whom can I talk to when things get overwhelming?

Taking Breaks, Taking Vacations

Entrepreneurs can be obsessive about their businesses. After all, the food on the table probably comes from the business. Also, small business owners invest emotionally in what they do and their success. It's not surprising that entrepreneurs need to develop the discipline to not work, either by taking breaks during the day or by taking work-free vacations. Here are some phrases to help avoid being all work and no play.

- It is important to me to take regularly scheduled days off from my business.
- I deserve a regular vacation.
- I recognize the value of maintaining a good balance between work and play.
- I listen to my family and friends when they tell me that I'm working too hard.
- I trust my family and friends to tell me I need to take a breather.
- I try to take a break from my business on legal holidays.
- If I do work on the weekends, I start later and finish earlier than I do on regular workdays.
- Part of my workday includes catching up with my family at mealtime.
- I make it a habit to break for 15 minutes with my kids when they arrive home from school.
- I use my alarm clock to remind me that it's time to "close up shop."
- When I take vacations, I pledge to myself and my family that I will not bring work material along, including my laptop or other electronic umbilical cords.

Challenging Yourself and Setting Goals

Taking on small business challenges and setting goals are normal for entrepreneurs. There will always be challenges, but the degree to which you take them on is up to you. You can determine your optimal risk levels from understanding which challenges and risks are comfortable for you and which are not, so you should have an idea about what motivates you and what may "freeze you like a deer in the headlights." Further, while it may seem unnecessary to set formal goals for yourself, it's advisable to do so. Write them down. Think about your levels of risk tolerance. Set goals. These phrases may help you.

- I understand that more difficult tasks motivate me more than easier tasks.
- When faced with relatively easy tasks only, I tend to "raise the stakes" for each task by setting an aggressive completion date or time.
- When faced with relatively easy tasks only, I look for other creative ways to "raise the stakes" for each task.
- I ensure that my goals are relevant to my business success.
- I am proud to say that I always meet my business commitments.
- I am fully committed to doing business according to my personal values and moral compass.
- I stay updated with trends, innovations, and global events that affect my business by reading, listening to audio books, and attending seminars.
- I believe that often there is more than one correct solution

to a problem and usually seek out at least three different solutions.

- When the need arises to deliver difficult news, I do so clearly and compassionately in a timely manner.
- I challenge myself and my employees to ensure that mistakes made are never repeated.
- I challenge myself and my employees to ensure that successes are not only repeated, but always improved upon.
- My personal mission statement states how I can positively influence my family and community, as well as stating my personal goals.
- I reserve the right to challenge the adage, "The best way to predict someone's future actions is to examine that person's past actions."
- I view failures as temporary situations and the best teaching tools.

Positive Self-Talk

Psychologists have discovered that how we talk to ourselves internally, our self-talk, as it reflects what we believe, can affect how we think and how we behave. So you can impact your mind-set by what you say to yourself, and a number of psychologists are now using cognitive behavior modification to help people do this. It's a therapeutic technique in which people challenge the beliefs and assumptions that are causing them to be unhappy and unsuccessful.

A short positive self-talk can help you overcome barriers and setbacks in your business, but it's important that self-talk not be based in a fantasy world. It needs to be at least somewhat based on your reality, or else you will delude yourself and make poor decisions.

- I do not accept the word "cannot" as part of my business vocabulary.
- Replace the phrase "I cannot . . . " with "I can . . . . "
- My hard work will pay off for me and my family.
- I believe in my unique skills and assets.
- My belief in my skills and talents will allow me to earn trust and respect from potential clients.
- I have a great service/product that's beneficial to clients.
- I expect good things to happen.
- In the unexpected, I can find the positive.
- I embrace change and challenges.
- I am in charge of my future.
- I am proud of what I have accomplished today.

Staying Focused and Improving Concentration

Particularly when stressed, we all have the tendency to avoid what we need to do or to distract ourselves or to otherwise lose focus and concentration. Here are a few questions you can ask that will bring you closer to techniques to stay focused and improve your concentration.

- Do I have too many distractions (such as television, refrigerator, family activities) where I work?
- Do I use music effectively to improve my concentration?
- Is the lighting in my workspace allowing me to stay focused?
- Can I recognize when my concentration is waning?
- Do I have a proven method to help me stay focused?
- Can I tell when my lack of focus means that I should take a break from work?
- Is there a time-sensitive task I should be completing rather than working on this particular task, and am I allowing this fact to distract me?
- Is this a good time to suspend this task for the day and work on tasks that are less critical?
- Does this task or project contribute to the success of my business?
- Am I using this task as a way to procrastinate delivering bad news to a client or an employee?

Staying Energized

The demands on a small business owner or operator are such that it's important to monitor and manage your energy levels. As you age, you may find it even more important to do so, so you have a reserve to deal with unexpected and demanding tasks and issues. Maintaining an even level of energy is much smarter than pushing yourself to exhaustion and then having to rest for days before becoming productive again, and it's far easier and healthier over the long run. Here are some phrases to help you stay energized.

- I surround myself with enthusiastic and positive people.
- I maintain a healthy lifestyle.
- I do not allow petty grievances to dominate my life.
- I am happy with my life so far.
- I live my life true to my values and beliefs.
- I practice stress-relieving strategies.
- I use my alone time to recharge my batteries.
- Spending time on my hobbies energizes me.
- I believe that scheduling regular times of quiet reflection is a good way to stay energized.
- I appreciate the simple moments in life.
- My sense of humor is one of my most important assets.
- I believe that my capacity for success is unlimited.

Staying Organized

Some people are naturally well organized, while others are exceedingly disorganized, while a third group uses "organizing" as an excuse for not doing real work. Obviously staying well organized can make you more efficient, provided you don't spend too much time on the organizing tasks, which do not directly result in additional revenue.

That said, effective organization will reduce your stress levels and help you feel efficient and productive, so staying well organized has a positive effect on your mental state. Try the following phrases.

- I keep and update a "must do" list of tasks and projects that are most urgent and most important.
- I keep and update a "must do" list of tasks and projects that are important, but not urgent.
- I keep and update a "want to do" list of tasks and projects that I want to complete.
- I keep and update a "would like to do" list of tasks and projects that I will want to complete in the future.
- My first task of every workday is to take a few minutes to plan my day or to review my day's plan.
- I use a daily planner and always keep it at hand.
- I always plan for the unexpected and unanticipated (such as traffic tie-ups or flight delays).
- I use color-coded file folders to denote the status of each of my major projects (e.g., blue = in progress, green = not yet started, red = complete).

- At the end of my workday, I always leave my workspace clear and organized.
- I have an organized system for storing business cards that I receive.
- My business card storage system includes information for each card, such as where I met the person and some initial thoughts on how we may develop a mutually beneficial business relationship.
- I schedule routine business maintenance tasks regularly (such as filing, ordering supplies, inventorying supplies, and maintaining my Web site).

Being Realistic About Setbacks

If you don't experience business setbacks, you probably are simply not noticing them (which could be good), since all businesses have ups and downs, particularly small ones and start-ups. If you let setbacks discourage you or push you into giving up, then maybe you should give up or simply just not start. Expect challenges—and be realistic and ready for them.

- This is my first year in business, and my market research indicated that this time of year is typically not busy.
- According to previous years, profits at this time of year shrink.
- What can I learn from this setback?
- How can I prevent losing another client because of this issue?
- This sort of setback is expected in my type of business.
- This is a good time to reevaluate the longevity of this particular product.
- This is a good lesson to remember.
- What changes, if any, are necessary to my business plans?
- I have to think about how to regain my customers' trust and reliance.
- How can I make this situation right for my client and prevent him or her from doing business with my competitor?
- Mistakes tend to provide more learning opportunities than performing perfectly.
- Did this setback arise because I've lost heart for the business?

Rewarding Yourself

We all need feedback, recognition, and rewards for the effort and sacrifices we make to push our businesses to succeed. We get some feedback from our bottom lines and our customers, and we get additional feedback and recognition from those around us, particularly family and friends.

That's important, but it's also important to learn to pat yourself on the back for a job well done or a success. Enjoy your triumphs, and take time to celebrate accomplishments before moving on to your next challenge. Provide positive feedback to yourself. Consider rewarding yourself frequently, in simple and inexpensive ways.

- I have proved to myself that I am a good businessperson.
- My business success so far tells me that going into business for myself was a great choice.
- I deserve a half-hour break; I think I'll treat myself to a cappuccino at the bakery.
- My presentation went really well this morning. I think I'll call Bill and see if he would like to meet for a quick lunch.
- This order brings me over my monthly quota, and we're still early in the month. Before I start filling the order, I'll take a break and think about what to do with the extra income.
- My profits exceeded my projections this year; I'm going to share the extra income with my employee(s).
- I've lowered my business costs by 15 percent. I'll use the savings to upgrade my computer systems.
- I've worked hard these past two years to stabilize my business; now is a good time to hire competent managers and assistants.

Guiding Principles

You are responsible for arranging your life and your thoughts so you can function optimally and deal effectively with the demands of operating a small business.

Stay positive but realistic. Living in a fantasyland about your business is not healthy, and it doesn't usually work long term.

Managing yourself and your energy and motivational levels as you run your business is much like managing yourself as an athlete or a performer. There's a "mental game" that you must address consciously.

It's easy to neglect self-management when operating a business that has the potential to take infinite amounts of work. Step back (perhaps at least once a day) to evaluate how you are managing yourself.

Chapter 6
Personnel, Hiring, and Policies

Small business owners and operators often have to do important tasks that would be delegated to human resources experts. Hiring, managing personnel, and formulating policy are examples. The alternative to undertaking personnel functions yourself is to outsource or hire a consultant.

Whether you do it yourself or hire an expert, you need to understand the basics. We've included phrases that will help you better understand some aspects of the human resources function.

Before you continue, you must ask yourself the following question: Do I understand enough about hiring and employment laws in this jurisdiction to safely manage the HR functions for my business? If you make human resources decisions without knowledge of the law, you open yourself up to lawsuits that can cripple your business. Consider having a personnel expert review what you are doing, at minimum.

Writing a Job Description

The job description serves several purposes. It can be used:

- As a basis for hiring
- To compare positions to determine salaries
- To communicate responsibilities to both new and established employees
- As a basis for evaluating job performance

Writing job descriptions forces you to think about the kinds of tasks you need completed by your employees and helps you determine the qualifications you need in the people you hire. Note that a job description is both a public document (written to be read by people outside the company) and a private one (used for internal purposes).

Keep in mind that no job description will accurately capture every single part of a job, so you want to tread a path between being too general, which results in providing little information of value, and being too specific, which results in descriptions that will go on for page after page or become quickly outdated.

We can think of the job description as containing a job title, a summary of the job (sometimes including the relationship of the job to other jobs in the company), duties and responsibilities, and requirements. If you're using the job description to fill a position, you could also include the salary and any benefits and, as a requirement, the time when you need the new hire to start. We've provided you with example phrases for each of these parts of the job description.

Job Title

- Senior Mechanic
- Entry-Level File Clerk
- Restaurant Manager
- Retail Store Stock Clerk (part time)
- Insurance Salesperson

Job Description

- Reporting to the store manager, the sales clerk is responsible for handling the cash and making store customers feel welcome.
- The chief Web designer develops and maintains the company Web site and provides Web design consulting advice and services to our external customers.
- Working within tight deadlines, the sales representative is responsible for meeting and working with prospective customers to sell high-value computer software.

Job Duties and Responsibilities

Be as specific as possible. This will spare you a lot of micromanaging.

- Open up store each morning at 8:30.
- Close up store each evening.
- Ring up purchases on Healey-Jones electronic cash register, and process payments in cash or by debit or credit card.
- Keep retail shelves clean, neat, and properly stocked.
- Produce complete Web design proposals for prospective customers.
- Design e-commerce Web sites to interact with online payment portals.

- Provide telephone assistance to customers with problems related to computer purchases from us.
- Diagnose and fix computer hardware and software problems.
- Provide orientation to new patients.
- Provide reassurance to and be a calming influence with first-time counseling clients.

Job Qualifications/Requirements

- Able to lift 30-pound boxes
- Available for evening and shift work
- Safe, accident-free driving record for last five years
- One year's experience as retail checkout clerk, preferably in a small clothing store
- Community college certificate in social work assistance program and/or bachelor's degree in a social science
- Able to work without supervision
- Two years' experience supervising junior-level restaurant staff
- One year of successful selling experience in an insurance brokerage or similar setting
- Available to start work immediately (or state date)
- Able to deal with distraught clients
- Thrives on aggressive deadlines
- Required to work on-call two weekends a month
- Willing to travel outside state on a monthly basis
- Minimum of one year's retail experience on checkout/cash register
- Licensed in New York State as a real estate agent
- Community college certificate in auto mechanics

- One year's experience in handling restaurant inventory and supplies and supervising employees

Salary and Benefits

- Yearly salary range $25,000–$30,000, based on experience and education, with potential for increase to $35,000 after one year.
- Base salary is $18,000 per year plus generous commission and health benefits.
- Pay is $8.00 per hour plus overtime rate for over 40 hours per week.
- Straight commission plus bonuses for hitting sales targets.
- Potential to increase earnings 20 percent through profit-sharing plan.

Writing Help Wanted Ads

Your help wanted ad serves a number of purposes. It must attract the attention of people qualified for the job. It must attract the best people possible, while not attracting those who are not qualified or whom you simply wouldn't want to hire. In other words, you want to get someone who can do the job right, and you want to do it as efficiently as possible, not wasting time with applications from people who are not qualified.

The solution is to provide enough information for the reader to make an informed decision whether to apply or not. Of course, you must ensure that your ad conforms to federal, state, and local laws governing discrimination.

Much of your want ad content can be taken from a job description if you have one already, although you may need to make some changes in wording or to shorten it so it fits within the ad space. In addition to job tasks, job requirements, and salary, which you can take from the job description, you can use the following phrases written specifically for job ads.

JOB DESCRIPTION

The job description in your ad should give a quick overview of the industry, type of company, and any other basic information (location, reporting relationship, type of customers/clients, etc.). This is similar to the job description you would write for your internal document, except that it includes information about the business that would be necessary for outsiders.

- Small retail crafts shop in South Shore, Chicago requires store clerk to serve customers, operate cash register, and track inventory.

- Busy family restaurant in SoHo, New York requires waiters and waitresses for both day and night shifts. Perfect for New York City students.

- Two-person book publishing firm requires experienced copy editor to edit/proof manuscripts and communicate about book proposals with authors.

- Small Web site design company requires a Web designer experienced in HTML, Java, JavaScript, and Flash to service current customers and maintain their business Web sites.

- Growing Web site design company seeks graphic/Web site designer to sell design services to small business, design Web sites, and do proposals for prospective customers.

- Psychological counseling office in downtown area requires person to provide clerical support to counselors during day shift.

- Cat Kennel in Dayton requires person to care for animals and serve pet owners.

STATEMENT OF JOB SELLING POINTS

Applicants are competing for the job you advertise, but also you are competing against other employers to attract applicants. It's important to remember that you need to grab the attention of people who are qualified for your job and entice them to apply. You need to include reasons. Why would someone want to work for you?

- Opportunity for top-quality person to advance to store manager position within one year.

- Ideal for individual wanting to work 20 hours a week.
- Entry-level job is ideal for recent college graduates.
- Job site is located close to public transportation.
- Work with a dedicated, fun team in a service-oriented industry.
- Opportunity to acquire counseling skills by learning from staff.
- Opportunity to make a difference in your community.
- Superior benefits and health coverage.
- Flexible work hours.
- Employee discount for permanent employees.
- Opportunity for animal lover to care for pets.

APPLICATION PROCEDURES

Tell prospective applicants how you want them to apply and whatever you don't want them to do. This helps everyone save time and avoid frustration. Be aware that no matter how clear your instructions, some people will not follow them.

- Please apply with resume, one-page cover letter, and three employment references by mail to [mailing address]. Your application must be postmarked by June 30, 20___.
- Sorry, no telephone or e-mail inquiries.
- You can e-mail your application to [e-mail address].
- E-mail, fax, or mail your application.
- Please drop off your application at our store between 2 p.m. and 6 p.m. before June 30, 20___.
- Sorry. Only applicants chosen for interviews will be contacted.
- We will confirm receipt of your application via e-mail if you provide us with your e-mail address.

Selecting for Interviewing

When jobs are in short supply, you may receive many applications—far too many to interview each applicant. How do you choose whom to interview? There's no scientific way to cull job applications, but we suggest using a systematic process, such as the following:

- Decide how many candidates you want to interview.
- Choose the three most critical qualifications, or characteristics you want in your employee.
- Quickly go through the pile of applications, and eliminate any applicants who lack the three critical qualifications.
- If you have too few candidates left, start over, but reduce the number of qualifications to two.
- If you have too many candidates, repeat the process, but add additional criteria.

Interviewing for Hiring

The better you are at interviewing job applicants, the more likely you are to find one who fits your needs (and vice versa). However, even experienced human resources professionals face challenges interviewing and choosing candidates. There are entire books to help you develop your interviewing skills. Here we're going to focus on a particular kind of questioning, which encourages the applicant to tell you how he or she has handled job situations in the past. The following phrases are general.

- Why do you want to work as a [job title]?
- What's your greatest strength related to this job, do you think?
- Where would you like to be in your career in five years?
- Are you comfortable with the starting salary, knowing that we'll review and increase it after you succeed in the six-month probation period?
- What did you like most about your previous job? What did you like least?
- Can you tell me why you've changed jobs three times in the past 12 months?
- Why did you leave your last position (or why do you want to leave)?

The phrases below are more specific and intended to explore both attitudes and skills.

- Can you give me an example of an accomplishment in your work history that made you proud?
- What is your proudest work accomplishment?

- Can you give me an example of how you have dealt with an angry customer successfully?
- Tell me about a failure you've had and how you overcame it.
- Tell me about a very high-pressure work situation and how you handled it.
- How have you faced a customer who was abusive? What did you do?
- Think about when you had a conflict with a coworker in a previous job. What did you do?
- In the past, when you were typing a memo for your boss, what did you do if the memo was full of spelling or grammatical errors?
- Think of a situation where you were successful in overcoming resistance and objections from a customer. What did you do to make the sale?
- In the past how have you used up-selling as part of your sales improvement strategy?
- How have you contributed to developing a sense of team in your previous jobs? How did that work out?

Communicating with Applicants

How you communicate with applicants affects how your company is perceived. If you interact badly with applicants, the word can get out and affect your ability to attract the applicants you want, because your reputation will suffer. Also, the news can get around to customers, too.

The basic principle is this: Ensure that you are interacting professionally and providing enough specific information to applicants, but do not waste time with communication that is unnecessary. Balance your need for efficiency with their need to know what is going on.

There are several points at which you may choose to communicate with applicants or when you must communicate:

- To acknowledge that you've received his or her application
- To notify the applicant that you are not interested in hiring him or her
- To arrange an interview
- To notify the applicant that you wish to hire him or her
- To finalize the employment agreement

Many companies no longer acknowledge receipt of an application, because they receive too many applications. It's still polite to respond on receipt. If you choose not to, you should mention that in your want ad.

When informing an applicant that you will not be making him or her an offer, be polite but short and to the point.

It's probably not wise to go into any detail about why you made that decision, due to potential legal issues, except to say that there were many highly qualified applicants.

If you choose to arrange an interview, it's best to contact the applicant by phone at a time that is convenient for both parties. You can also use e-mail.

If you decide to hire a person, inform him or her as soon as possible by phone or e-mail. It's always better to phone.

You may need to meet with your new hire prior to the first day of employment to finalize the employment agreement and to get to know each other. At this point, you will answer questions; provide more information about the job, benefits, and expectations; and sign any documents.

Here are additional phrases you can use in communicating with applicants, both in writing and orally.

- Thank you for your application. We will contact you within two weeks if we decide to interview you.
- Thank you for your application. We have hired another applicant, but we will keep your application on file for six months.
- We are unable to offer you a position at this time. However, feel free to apply if you see another advertisement from our company.
- We would like to have you come in for an interview. Are you available this Thursday, the 16th?
- Please bring a copy of your resume and a list of your references to the interview.
- You will be meeting with me and Mr. O'Connor, the co-owner. We expect to take an hour.

- Congratulations! We'd like to offer you the job.
- We are pleased that you will be coming to work here. We look forward to having you join our team. Can we set up a meeting to finalize the details?
- While we were impressed with your qualifications and resume, we received many outstanding applications and we are unable to hire you at this time.

Writing Policies

If you only have one or two employees, it may seem odd to take the time to write formal policies regarding their employment. There are several reasons to do so. First, a set of policies will help you be consistent with your employees over time. Second, written policies add an extra layer of protection for both the employer and the employee if there are disagreements. If you are sued regarding an employment issue, the court will consider your policies and the degree to which you followed them. Having policies in writing may even discourage frivolous lawsuits, particularly if you ask employees to sign a document indicating they have read the policies.

Below are examples of topics you might include in your policies and some phrasing you can customize.

- Employees will accrue vacation time at a rate of one day per month, starting on the first day of employment.
- During the first two years of employment, employees will receive two weeks of vacation per calendar year. After the first two years, employees will receive three weeks per year.
- Vacations must be taken at a time mutually acceptable to both employee and employer.
- Employees will accrue sick leave at the rate of three-fourths of a day for each month of employment.
- Employees are hired on a probationary basis for the initial six months.
- Employees are expected to dress to project a positive image to customers and coworkers.

- No body piercings, tattoos, or messages on clothing can be displayed during regular work hours.
- Overtime will be determined on the basis of [cite relevant laws]. Pay for overtime will be [state].
- Work-related expenses [itemize eligible expenses] will be reimbursed provided they have been preapproved (if over $100) and proper receipts are provided.
- Our standard workday begins at 8:30 a.m. and ends at 4:30 p.m., with a one-hour lunch from noon to 1:00 p.m. and mid-morning and mid-afternoon breaks of 15 minutes.

Guiding Principles

When you create personnel-related documents only for your own internal use, you can be somewhat flexible about what you include and how you phrase them.

Above all else, your personnel-related documents need to conform to federal, state, and local labor and equity laws in your jurisdiction. To ignore this is to invite problems if you employ even one person.

If you develop policies in writing, you need to abide by them. Your policies are rules and guidelines for employees, but they obligate you to follow them.

Treat employees and potential employees with respect and consideration. If you mistreat them, word gets around, and it can negatively affect your customers and potential customers—a problem that is particularly serious for small businesses.

Chapter 7
Employee Orientation
and Training

No matter whom you hire (or who works for/with you) and how skilled and competent the employee might be, you can't expect him or her to know how you want the job done, how to fit into the company, and what's important and less important. A new employee must be oriented to your business, since each business is in some ways unique.

In addition, you can't expect any employee to know everything required to do the job without your help, coaching, and training. The investment you make in both new and current employees to help them get up to speed and develop their skills will pay off over and over again, in better performance, less staff turnover, and fewer demands on you to manage employees. This applies whether you're working with relatives or with relative strangers.

In this chapter we'll cover aspects of employee orientation and training.

Orientation: Welcoming New Employees (First Day)

As the business owner/operator, you should make a point of being available to spend some time with a new employee on his or her first day of employment. You serve two functions: to make the employee feel welcome, valued, and comfortable and to familiarize the employee with his or her job and how things are done in the company. Here's a range of phrases you can use in welcoming new employees.

- John, welcome to Smitty's. I've put aside some time to show you around and give you an overview of your job and the layout of things around here.

- Mary, I'm Bob Medavoy, the owner of the business. While you are going to be working for Evelyn in sales, I'd like to show you around. Then Evelyn can fill you in on your specific responsibilities and introduce you to the people you'll be working with.

- Since this is a two-person business, you and I will be working together closely, so let's take some time to get to know each other. I'll show you around, and then I'll take you out to lunch.

- Before we sit down, let me show you around the office, so you'll know where everything is.

Orientation: Job Expectations and Company Culture

An employee will fit in better and be more productive if he or she knows how things are done in your office and what you expect of him or her. A major part of formal and informal orientation involves conveying a sense of the culture of the organization and its formal and informal rules. The period of formal orientation, which usually occurs as soon as the employee starts the job, is short. On the other hand, the informal orientation continues over a long time.

Educating employees is part of your job, and it's an ongoing responsibility. Here are some phrases that can be used to communicate about job expectations and culture.

- Around here, it's important that we be available to our customers when we say we will be. We aren't sticklers about being on time, but please be here during our core hours.

- If you have a question or problem, it's best to talk to your supervisor, who's going to be training you. If she can't help, the three of us can meet.

- I expect that my employees will work together and get along with each other as team members. You may not like everyone, but I expect professional team conduct.

- Some places set deadlines and then don't meet them. We're not like that. If there's a deadline, treat it very seriously.

- Once you get settled, I hope you'll be able to take on more authority and make more decisions on your own.

- I believe in balancing work and non-work life, particularly family, so I'm not going to ask you to work extra hours unless it's an absolute emergency.

Training: Explaining

Training is about helping your employees do their jobs more effectively, more productively, and the way you want. It may be up to you or someone to whom you delegate the task to ensure the employee has the skills, knowledge, and understanding needed to do the job. As the job changes, new skills may be required. It's your job to make sure your employees develop and use them.

Training can be done in a number of different ways, but we're going to use a simple model that includes these steps:

- Tell and explain.
- Demonstrate.
- Have the employee practice and then give you feedback about how well he or she did.
- Coach and tweak as needed.

It's important you recognize that training is not just telling and explaining. Instructions are a part of training, but only a small part of making sure each employee has the skills needed. In this section we'll provide some phrases that exemplify good explanations and instructions. In the subsequent sections, we'll do the same for the rest of the instructional/training process.

- Mary, I need you to make sure that you are here each morning by 8 a.m. to open up the store and to turn off the alarm. I've written out the instructions for you.
- When you access our computer network, you'll have to set up a password for yourself that has at least 10 numbers or letters, with at least two of those being numbers.

- When you wrap client purchases, make sure to package the fragile objects together and use bubble wrap and to use boxes for bulkier objects.
- Each shipment includes the product the customer ordered plus a shipping slip and notification of credit card payment, if that's the way the customer paid.
- We'd like you to answer the phone with our company name and then ask, "How may I help you?"

Training: Demonstration and Practice

One of the most powerful ways to teach someone how to do a job is to demonstrate so the person can see the job done properly. However, some demonstrations are good, and some are less effective. Demonstrate correctly, and your employee will learn faster. Here are some phrases which exemplify effective use of demonstration in conjunction with providing the chance for employees to practice what you have described, then demonstrated.

- John, I'm going to demonstrate how I'd like you to deal with a credit card transaction. I'll break it down for you in a moment, but first I'll show you the whole thing, so just watch.

- First, I'm going to get the credit card from the client. I'll run the card through the scanner, input the proper amount, output the receipt for the customer to sign, and then compare the receipt signature with the signature on the back of the card.

- Now, let's go through the first step. I take the card from the customer, thank her, and run the card through the scanner. Now, imagine I'm the customer. Try it with me.

- Good. Now let's move to the next step. Watch how I .... [Describe what you are doing as you demonstrate.]

- Now I'll show you the final step. Again, watch to see how I .... [Explain while showing.] Then you can try it.

- That's basically the whole process. You've done each step, one by one. Now let's see if you can do the whole sequence. I'll walk you through it verbally the first time.

- OK. Good. Now, try it again, but this time without me guiding you.

Training: Practice and Feedback

Feedback involves providing information about how well an employee has done, either during practice or on the job, and includes specifics about what the employee should continue doing and what should be changed.

Feedback needs to be immediate (closely associated in time with whatever is the focus of your feedback), specific, related to the performance, and reasonable. An employee cannot learn if he or she is overwhelmed by a dump of details. You have to be both patient and reasonable, accepting the fact that not everything can be learned immediately and that what is simple to you, the expert, is not simple to someone new to it. Here are phrases that exemplify proper use of feedback during training, based upon employee practice.

- That's great, John. During our role play, you welcomed me to the shop and processed my payment using the correct sequence we talked about.

- Mary, you seemed a bit stiff and tense when we practiced this, so let's try it again. Try to relax and have fun with it.

- You looked a little worried when you entered the data into the computer. Remember: You can't damage the machine by anything that you do, so no need to worry about that.

- That's excellent. You did each of the steps individually just as they need to be done. Now, let's try something a bit more difficult.

- Did you notice that when you pressed the escape key, the file closed? Good. The problem is that if you exit that way, you won't retain any of your changes, which is why you need to always exit using the exit menu. Make sense?

■ I like the way you arranged the flowers so there was a balance of small and large ones in the bouquet, but you might want to try to coordinate the colors a bit better. For example, you could try ....

Buddying Up or Shadowing

A modified way of helping an employee learn, particularly if he or she is going to do tasks that you do, is to have the person accompany you or watch you as you complete the tasks. For example, if you go on sales calls and have just hired a salesperson, you might have that person come along on your calls to watch how you do it. Not only does this help build skills, but it shows the employee how you want things done.

However, going along to watch isn't enough to ensure learning, so you need to set up the learning process properly. Here are examples that illustrate the proper use of shadowing.

■ When we meet with our client, I'll introduce you, but I'd like you to stay on the sidelines and just watch what I do. Next time we go out, I'll let you take on part of the meeting.

■ When we meet with the supplier, watch how I spend a few minutes talking about his family and catching up. That's to form good personal relationships. You might want to try that when you go out on your own.

■ When we go out on deliveries, I map out the most efficient delivery route. You'll need to be doing that too, or you won't get the deliveries done in time.

■ Did you notice how I dealt with the customer's initial objections by mentioning how much she'd save over the long run? People are interested in long-term savings even when they focus on the short term.

■ What did you see me do during the training session with that trainee who kept interrupting?

■ Why do you think I did that?

- Can you think of other ways I could have handled the person who keeps interrupting?
- Did you notice that during the meeting Mary seemed upset? That's why I asked for a coffee break, so I could talk with her privately and put her fears at rest.

Setting Up Other Learning Activities

While it's a good idea for you to be involved in training employees, particularly so they know how you want things done, you don't have to provide all of the learning activities directly. There are a number of ways employees can learn and develop using other resources. In this section we'll present some phrases and questions that relate to alternative ways to supplement employee learning and development.

- John, I've showed you the basics of the computer software, but there's a lot more. On this shelf here are the manuals, and there's a tutorial disk. I'd like you to do the tutorial by next Friday. Then on Friday we'll get together and discuss what you've learned.

- Mary, you've been doing a great job over the last year, and the business is expanding. We plan on creating a managerial position and would like to see you develop your supervisory skills. Would you like to attend an evening course or two at the community college?

- Your coworkers know a lot about how to [whatever], so I've asked them to spend some time each day with you helping you get up to speed. If you have any questions, you can ask your coworkers as you work together.

- What kind of things do you feel you need to learn to do your job more effectively? We'll see whether we can find some resources for you.

- There's a seminar coming up on designing business brochures. Since you've expressed interest in taking on new, creative assignments, I thought you might like to attend.

Employee Orientation and Training

- We like our staff to be constantly learning, so we will pay up to $400 a year for job-related training. If you would like to take advantage of this, let me know.
- I encourage staff to take at least 10 minutes each day browsing the newspaper to keep up with current events, since our customers like to talk about what's going on.
- I encourage our employees to take at least an hour or two a week reading journals related to our business, so feel free to do so when things are slow.

Guiding Principles

Training is a shared responsibility. As owner/operator, you need to be involved both in teaching employees how you want things done and what you expect of them, as well as in giving them a sense of the culture of the organization.

There are many cheaper and effective alternatives to training seminars and courses. You need not spend huge amounts of money on training. Get employees involved in finding resources for learning and training.

Training and learning need to be ongoing, not just for new employees. Not only does that help your business grow, but it is also stimulating for employees to learn new things.

Certain kinds of training may be mandated or required by law. You should become familiar with federal laws governing employment. Since there are also state and local laws, it's smart to contact your state department of labor to find out about workplace safety and health requirements and any other requirements for employers.

Chapter 8
Leadership, Employee Motivation, Work Climate, and Credibility

As a small business owner or operator, it's your responsibility to provide a climate in which your employees can thrive. You need your employees to want to do a good job, and you want them to feel part of something important and meaningful. These things don't happen magically. They develop through strong leadership from you. If you create such a climate by establishing your own credibility, helping employees to understand how and why their contributions are important, and treating people well, your gains will be huge. Well-motivated employees who are "on board" or "engaged" require much less supervision and management, take initiative if allowed, and are more productive.

Leadership is a bit of a mystery, and there's no universal formula to follow. However, there are some elements that are well established as being important in fostering a productive, healthy, and positive workplace.

Communicating Values, Mission, and Vision

You may recall we talked about values, mission, and vision in the chapter on writing a formal business plan. Here we're going to talk about these elements with respect to fostering employee commitment and engagement. After all, how can employees feel motivated to pursue your business mission or vision if they don't know what it is? How can employees act in ways consistent with your business's values if they don't know what they are? Here are some examples of phrases that you can use with employees relative to your values, mission, and vision.

■ We are in the business of launching senior citizens on their second career.

■ We provide seniors with the tools to find their true calling in today's workforce.

■ Our aim is to ensure that those experienced employees who wish to remain working can do so effectively long after the traditional retirement age.

■ Complaining customers are turned into satisfied customers through our commitment to training employees to handle difficult or angry customers.

■ Commitment to our vision helps everyone pull in the same direction.

■ We will always try to act consistent with our vision and values as a company.

■ Our values are our guide.

■ All of us—employees and owner—represent the values, mission, and vision of our company to the world.

- Our shared mission is to improve business communications with seminars and customized reading materials in order to help employees become articulate at all levels.
- As a representative of this company, I believe we are better than our competitors, and I can tell potential clients why and how we are better.

Living and Demonstrating Values and Vision

Far more important than verbal statements of values or vision is the leader's ability to demonstrate the application of values and vision through action. You must live the values and vision you want employees to commit to.

No amount of words will gain commitment to values and vision if leaders don't live them consistently each and every day. Here are some examples of phrases that show how this can sound in various contexts.

- John, around here we don't bully each other, verbally or otherwise.
- Mary, we've all agreed to share resources and not to compete with each other, so next time, could you put back the files and promo material quickly so others can use them?
- Not only are we going to figure out bonuses on the basis of individual sales, but we'll also take into account the total success of the company. So when we succeed, we succeed together.
- How does your decision bring us closer to realizing our vision of this company?
- I think your suggestion is great, but does it distract us from the primary purpose of our business?
- If our primary concern is customer satisfaction, how can you contribute more fully to achieving that?
- Fred, are there any jobs you want to take on that are consistent with the goals we've set for next year?
- I want to get your input and ideas on this. I promise you I'll look at them to see which ones we can do and get back to you.

Encouraging Participation and Engagement

Employee "participation" and "engagement" are not just buzz words consultants throw at business owners. While these terms may be trendy, there is value in making the effort to encourage participation and input and to engage employees to act on behalf of the business, their teammates, and themselves.

Apart from improving employee morale, participation has value because the people most able to solve business problems are usually the folks on the front lines—your employees. They know the flaws and good points of how you do business, and they often know how to fix things—if only someone with formal authority would ask them or help them feel comfortable participating.

Here are some perfect phrases for encouraging employee participation and engagement.

- Let me remind everyone that the main focus of brainstorming during the initial phase is to list as many ideas as possible without debate or any need for consensus. There are no wrong ideas.

- Let's remember that the intrinsic value of any idea is the other ideas that it may inspire.

- A true team is one where all members participate in discussions and all are truly engaged in the subject at hand.

- I'm interested in hearing what you think, Bob; you always bring a fresh perspective to the discussion.

- There is sure to be as many different opinions in this meeting as there are people; we need to hear from everybody in order to solve this problem so that we all benefit.

■ For the duration of this discussion, I'll ask everyone to stay on topic; to that end, I am asking for a volunteer to call out if we stray off the topic.

■ I value each of your opinions and insights.

■ If you have an idea about how to fix [business problem], please come visit me, even if you think the idea "might sound dumb."

■ I believe that a decision reached by consensus grows in value exponentially by the number of people involved in making the decision.

■ Your attention and dedication to the values of this company speak highly of your self-motivation.

■ I am proud of you as a team; each of you recognizes your own particular talent and respects each other's talents, and as a result, you all keep this company running at its peak.

■ What drives you nuts about working here?

■ Are there any procedures we use that don't make sense or that we can flat-out eliminate?

Inspiring and Motivating Employees Through Recognition

In real life, the things you do to engage employees and encourage participation are also the things you can do to inspire and motivate them. There's a lot of overlap. Here are some phrases to use in recognizing your employees.

- We can all learn from your attention to detail.
- You did a great job. I appreciate your efforts.
- I know I can always count on you to perform at your best.
- As a reward for your hard work, I can offer you time off with pay, or a cash bonus, or tickets to a major sporting event, or a gift certificate from your favorite store.
- You are a leader. Your leadership skills are showing. You lead others by influence.
- I'd like to have a fun, informal idea of the week, where I buy coffee for the person with the best productivity improvement idea during the week.
- Thanks to the two of you for getting the inventory done in record time and for not complaining about a really tedious job.

Credibility and Trust

Let's turn to the issues of credibility and trust. Employees who believe and trust you, your abilities, and your honesty and integrity will be much more likely to share your vision and to work hard and with great loyalty. The flip side, however, is that if you do things that send the message that you aren't trustworthy, you will struggle constantly with employee motivation problems, even if you hire new employees.

In this section we look at how you can address employee complaints and concerns in ways that will build your trustworthiness and credibility. We include phrases that you can use when intervening in conflicts or difficulties between employees.

ADDRESSING INTERNAL COMPLAINTS OR CONFLICTS

- Can you tell me about any actions you've taken to resolve this disagreement with James?
- Do you have a suggestion for handling this issue?
- What kind of help would you like from me to help solve this problem?
- You sound very frustrated about this. I would like you and Barry to sit down together to resolve your differences. Then you both can let me know if you think the three of us should meet.
- I agree that there is a better way of handling the situation. Let's discuss this with everyone impacted to determine a viable solution.
- Here's how I see the problem: … Here's how I would like

you to handle it: ... So let's meet in a few days to discuss whether further action is required.

- Tell me how you think you contributed to the escalation of this situation.

- Tell me how you think others contributed to the escalation of this situation.

- Tell me how you will handle this type of complaint in the future.

- We have a problem here that we need to resolve without delay. Let's get the problem under control before we change our policies and procedures.

COMPLAINTS ABOUT YOU

Employees watch how you handle conflicts with peers and employees, and they form opinions based on observing how you interact with others. One critical area is how you handle private and public complaints about you and your actions. The ideal is to provide a climate where people are free to constructively discuss your decisions and actions and to express their concerns to you, rather than discuss them behind your back.

- It sounds like you are upset. I'd like to hear what you have to say, even if it's about me.

- I'm willing to listen to your concerns, but let's agree that there won't be any profanity or yelling. OK?

- Even if you and I disagree, there may be some room for compromise so we both get closer to what we want.

- I'll try to accommodate your needs. But if I can't, I can understand why you might want to look for employment that is more satisfying.

- In a perfect world, what would you like me to do about this?
- I can't [insert whatever the person is asking you to do], but there are some options that might work here. I can ...
- I apologize if my words upset you. I did not mean them to be insulting, and they don't reflect a lack of confidence in you. I hope we can leave this behind.
- You are a valuable employee. We'll try to make you happy, but if we can't, please understand it's not personal.
- Thanks for coming directly to me on this. I know you are upset, but I'm happy you had the courage to come to me.

ADMITTING MISTAKES

Some misguided people believe a leader should never admit making a mistake. That's wrong. Employees don't trust those who try to come across as perfect—and for good reason. We all know that nobody is perfect, and we tend to see a refusal to admit mistakes as either obliviously stupid or dishonest. Neither of these perceptions creates trust. Here are some phrases worth considering when you realize you have made an error.

- I wholeheartedly apologize for my error in judgment.
- Here's how I intend to resolve the issue ...
- I thought it was the best action to take at the time. I am sorry that I didn't make a better decision.
- Here's how I can prevent a similar mistake ...
- I am sorry and want you to know that this mistake was a huge lesson for me.
- I made a mistake. I am sorry.
- I was wrong.

- I made an incorrect assumption.
- My understanding of the situation is incorrect.
- I am proof that performing a task perfectly is not as educational as goofing up can be.
- For every mistake made, a lesson is learned. For every task performed perfectly, a person remains unchanged.
- Thank you for pointing out that I missed a few things when making my decision.

HANDLING QUESTIONS YOU CAN'T ANSWER

None of us likes to think that others believe we're stupid, so we feel awkward when we are asked questions we cannot answer (either because we don't know or because we cannot divulge the answer). Attempting to fake it when answering tough questions will almost certainly result in the opposite of what you desire. The loss of trust and consequent damage to commitment and employee motivation will ensue. Here are a few perfect phrases for dealing with questions you cannot answer.

- I don't have an answer for you right now, but I will get back to you.
- I'm afraid I don't have an answer. Can anyone else shed some light on this question?
- That's a complicated question that requires a lot of thought and investigation. Let's table it and bring it up at our next meeting.
- Good question! I'll put it on my to-do list and be ready to discuss it with you next week.
- That is a question that I am not prepared to answer at this moment.

- This is a question for an expert on the subject. Let's engage a subject-matter expert to present a seminar for us.
- I don't have enough information on that subject to discuss it without sounding evasive, so I'll have to decline to answer at this time.
- I am not entirely sure of the answer. Let's set up a later meeting with this question as the sole agenda. Will someone volunteer to research this matter?
- The answer to this question requires at least an hour to explain fully. Let's schedule another meeting. If anyone else has questions on this matter, send them to me, and I will add them to the agenda.
- I may inadvertently have misled you, since I don't have enough information on that subject. Now that I know there is interest in this, I'll share the information as I learn more.

Guiding Principles

Leading, motivating, and developing a positive climate requires that you demonstrate what you want by being a role model. You can't just talk a good game. Your actions have to be consistent with your words.

The point of attending to the work environment and your employees is to have motivated, focused, and competent employees who require minimal supervision, no matter what size your business.

Credibility and trust are based on your words, your actions, the consistency between the two, your commitment to your employees' welfare, and your efforts to involve employees. All these will also have a huge influence on how employees feel and how hard they will work for you.

Spend time building trusting relationships with employees. The effort has real payoffs for the bottom line.

Chapter 9
Managing Employee Performance

Small business owners and operators tend to neglect an important responsibility—managing the performance of their employees in a systematic, organized, and planned way. What does this mean? The simplest way to put it is that managing performance involves creating an environment that will enable employees to perform their jobs as well as possible. The result can be optimal performance and less need for ongoing supervision, which frees up the owner or operator to do other things that only he or she can do.

Creating this environment involves several things. Generally, you must attend to all of them to maximize performance. We've organized examples for each component.

Setting Goals with Employees

Employees need to have goals that mean something to them. The best goals for employees are measurable and are expressed in terms of how much, how well, how good, and so on. When goals are measurable, you and the employee can use them to evaluate how well the employee has done. It's best to set goals together with employees, particularly if they are familiar with your business and have worked there for a while, but even new employees can participate in goal-setting discussions.

- Fred, this month our goal is to increase sales by 5 percent. What kind of goal could we set for you that will help you contribute to this overall increase?
- I'd like you to reduce the time you spend on each sales call without losing any sales. Can you think of a way to word a goal like that so it seems fair to you?
- You've demonstrated some leadership qualities, so I'd like to have you develop your supervisory skills during the next year.
- I notice you've been late a few times this month. Next month I'd like to see you arrive on time every time. I'll help if I can. Then I'd like to meet with you at the end of next month to see how you've done on this.
- The shelves you are responsible for should be clean, neat, and properly stocked at all times. I want you to make that your primary goal.
- I'd like to see you develop and implement at least one cost-saving idea applicable to your own work each year.

- One of the things I'd like to see happen is that you ensure that your actions don't interfere with coworkers or make them less productive.
- I expect that you will input data at a rate of at least 8,000 keystrokes per hour.

For more on performance goals, see *Perfect Phrases for Performance Goals* by Douglas Max and Robert Bacal (McGraw-Hill, 2002).

Giving Informal Feedback

Employees need to know how they are doing and whether they are performing up to your expectations. More specifically, they need to know what they are doing well and should keep doing. They also need to know what they are doing less well and how they might do it better. Luckily, in most small businesses, the owner or operator is in a position to get to know employees, observe how they're doing their jobs, and play a critical role in helping them improve.

Informal feedback should consist of both encouragement and specific comments on performance, and you should provide it frequently, spontaneously, whenever the occasion arises. You should be encouraging and emotionally supportive, but you should also be specific about what the employee should continue and what he or she should change and how.

Here are some sample perfect phrases that show how to provide informal feedback.

- Great job, Mary, dealing with that cranky customer. You empathized and calmed her down quickly, and then you made the sale.
- I heard from Jackie Smith, the customer you dealt with yesterday, and she's just glowing with praise. Good one!
- I have a quick suggestion for you. When a customer provides objections to the sale, let the person finish before responding. I've noticed you sometimes interrupt, which can put off a customer.

- Here's a tip. When you input data, you can use some keyboard shortcuts instead of the mouse, and that will make things go faster. Here, let me show you a few that can make your job easier.

- I noticed that you don't always check the signature on the back of the credit cards or you do it too quickly. It's really important that you check for each and every credit card transaction, since the credit card company will charge back payments if we don't check signatures.

- I noticed that with the last customer, you went along with her request to have her hair tinted blue, even though I'm sure you knew it was a bad idea. In the future, before going along with a bad idea, try suggesting some alternatives that might look better.

For more on giving feedback and performance reviews, see *Manager's Guide to Performance Reviews* by Robert Bacal (McGraw-Hill, 2003).

Doing Formal Evaluations

Formal evaluations, often called annual performance appraisals, are much less effective in helping employees improve their job performance than informal feedback on a regular basis. That's because formal evaluations come too infrequently and too long after the fact, not immediately after the behavior in question.

They still have value, though. They provide written records of communication about performance, problems, and strengths, documentation that can be used later on to make decisions about promotions, pay increases, or even layoffs and firings. Formal evaluations also offer some protection from accusations of illegal discrimination, provided they can document that employment decisions were made on the basis of job-related performance and not personal characteristics (e.g., gender, race, age, and so on), which would be illegal.

Here are some phrases you can use in formal evaluations of performance, either oral or written.

PHRASES TO EXPLAIN THE PROCESS

- Every X months you and I are going to sit down and discuss your performance—what you've done well and how you might improve.
- Not only are we going to discuss your job performance, but we'll talk about how I can do a better job helping you do your job better.
- We'll discuss things, and then I'll write up a brief summary of our discussion, which I'd like you to sign to indicate

you've read it. Signing it doesn't necessarily mean you agree with it all. In fact, if you don't agree, you can add any comments to express your perspective.

■ Next week I'd like to get together with you to discuss your progress toward the goals we set last month. Can you take some time and review your goals prior to our meeting?

PHRASES TO DESCRIBE EMPLOYEE PERFORMANCE

■ Satisfactorily achieved all major goals on time
■ Has negotiated several sales deals with customers so that each side wins
■ Completed redesign of our Web site per goals on time and within budget
■ Completed redesign of Web site according to all specifications, except for a one-month delay
■ Consistently deals with difficult customers effectively
■ Occasionally shows impatience with elderly customers
■ Has been 10 or more minutes late for work at least three times in January, missing several important calls
■ Has achieved assigned sales quota for each month
■ Has helped other salespeople achieve their quotas each month
■ Has marketed our Web site such that traffic has increased 50 percent in the last three months and Web-based sales have increased 20 percent
■ Has missed sales quotas in three of the last six months, by at least 10 percent
■ Effectively calms down angry customers
■ Has shown an ability to accurately diagnose client problems over the phone

PHRASES FOR DEALING WITH INADEQUATE PERFORMANCE

No employee is perfect, so there will be occasions to address performance inadequacies. It's important to deal with problems early and not to wait until they increase in frequency or severity. Standard procedure is that you deal with performance problems privately with the employee and as soon as you become aware of the problems.

You can use the following phrases as examples for discussions of relatively minor performance issues.

- Sharon, I've noticed that you've been late to open the office three times this month, and we've missed some important calls. Is there a problem that's been delaying your arrival?

- I'll be glad to help you plan your time a bit better so you can get here on time. Is there something I can help with?

- I've heard from Jack Patterson that you come across as brusque on the phone, and I've noticed that myself. We need to work on that, so I'd like to spend some time, just you and me, practicing some telephone skills.

- I can see your sales figures are down, and we need to get them back up again. I'll be glad to help you. I want to see an upward trend, at least, in the next month, or we'll have to do a more formal review of your performance.

- I think you get along very well with almost everyone here, but I've noticed a lot of friction and angry words between you and Freddy. I'm going to speak to Freddy also. I have the same message for both of you. You don't have to like each other, but I expect you will treat each other politely

and civilly. If you need to know what that means specifically, let me know.

■ There's some room for improvement here, and I want to
work with you to address the problem. If we can get your
numbers up by December, you'll get a nice 4 percent bonus.

PHRASES FOR DEALING WITH SERIOUS
PERFORMANCE PROBLEMS

There will be times when you will face much more serious
performance problems. Obviously what constitutes a serious problem will depend on your business, on your expectations, and on the effects of the problem. Some problems
are always serious. For example, an employee who steals is
committing an illegal act and is also attacking your bottom
line. That's serious. An employee may occasionally be rude
or impatient with a customer. Is that "serious"? You'll have
to decide.

However you define "serious," a serious performance
problem is something that you cannot allow to continue.
Either the problem gets resolved, or the employee can no
longer work for your business. In some cases, the problem is
so severe that a single instance is enough reason to fire the
employee.

Here are phrases you can use as examples in talking with
employees about more serious performance problems.

■ John, it's not acceptable to swear at a customer, no matter
what the provocation. Since you've been an asset to the
company and this is your first such incident, I'm going to
give you a formal warning. If this or something similar happens again, you'll be dismissed immediately.

- Mary, our security camera caught you removing money from the till last night. Unless you can provide me with a good explanation for what you were doing, I'll have to let you go.

- I know you've tried your best to develop the skills and reach the goals we set for you in January, but it looks like you might be better off and happier working for another company. I'm afraid we'll have to let you go. Let me explain how severance works and your options about finishing up your time with us.

- I'd be glad to write you a reference attesting to your reliability and friendliness.

- You've made some fairly serious mistakes that have caused us to lose two major customers. I'm willing to send you to appropriate training to address this problem, but if I hear we are losing another customer due to your errors, I'm going to have to terminate your employment.

- I want to let you know that you are on probation for the next three months. If we don't see improvement, specifically [insert target(s)], we'll have to let you go.

For more on performance management and performance appraisals, see *Performance Management* by Robert Bacal (McGraw-Hill, 1998) and *Perfect Phrases for Performance Reviews* by Douglas Max and Robert Bacal (McGraw-Hill, 2002).

Empowering Employees

There's a softer, more strategic side to managing employees and performance. Think about what you want from your employees. Do you want someone who needs to ask you before making even a minor decision? Or do you want someone who can make the right decision without having to ask? If you're smart, you'll want the latter, because it saves you time and aggravation and improves productivity.

The buzz word to describe employees who show initiative and make decisions is "empowered." Empowerment doesn't occur magically. You have to create it. Here are some phrases to show you how you can do that.

- I'd like you to take total control of this project. You can spend up to $1,000 without needing approval from me. Just keep in mind …

- Don't worry about doing things differently than I would. Achieve the goal we've set any way that makes sense and seems efficient.

- I'm going to fade into the background here, so you can deal with the client in your own way. If you need my help, you can ask. Otherwise, I won't be saying anything.

- Do you feel you are ready to take on making these kinds of decisions?

- Is there anything you need to know about the project so you'll feel comfortable making the project decisions?

- I'd like you to start taking on some of my management responsibilities with respect to [insert details]. How do you feel about that?

- What do you need from me so you can take over making decisions about pricing?
- Feel free to offer free merchandise to customers when we have messed up their orders and want to retain them as satisfied customers. Just limit the overall cost to $50.
- You have enough experience to have a sense where to put the various displays, so go ahead and set them up the way you think best. If I have any suggestions, I'll pass them on.
- Go ahead and use your own judgment. If you need my help to get the job done, let me know, and I'll try to clear away the barriers.

Delegating to Employees

Empowerment is about creating a climate where employees can make decisions autonomously, without consulting you. Delegation is similar in some respects, since it requires giving employees the power to carry out specific tasks. When you delegate, you give someone the authority and responsibility for a task that would normally be yours. For example, you might typically call customers to do some quick satisfaction interviews. This is something an employee could do on your behalf, provided that he or she knows the purpose of the calls and has the skills needed to do it successfully. When you delegate a task, you are also empowering the employee to make decisions and to do things his or her own way.

Here are some phrases that you can use as models when you delegate.

■ Mary, you've helped me order supplies a number of times, and we've talked about how to do it. I think you are ready to take on the responsibility on your own. How do you feel about that?

■ We're getting a lot of job applications. Since you've been here long enough to know what we need for the position, I'd like you to screen the job applications to weed out the applicants who are clearly unqualified. I'll give you the criteria to apply.

■ I'd like to send you to the meeting in my place, as my delegate, so you can speak for the company regarding the topic of [specify]. If other topics come up, I'd like you to consult me before making any commitment.

- What do you think you'd need to take on [job responsibility]?
- I want to be sure you're comfortable taking on my supervisory responsibilities when I'm not around, so let me know if you need help.
- You've done such a good job this year that I think you're ready for more. I don't want to punish you for doing so well, but are you interested in taking on the responsibility of . . . ?

Guiding Principles

Managing employee performance is as important as managing finances or inventory or customers, if not more important. Yet small business owners tend to neglect it. Invest in it for huge payoffs.

The core of performance management is communication, not fancy forms. When employees know what they need to achieve, understand how well they need to do their job tasks, and hear from you when they do well or need to change to do better, they can be far more productive.

Empowering employees and delegating to employees can allow you to have more time to focus on the aspects of the business that only you can address. Small business owners tend to have trouble letting go, but if you provide your employees with proper structure and guidelines and can tolerate some errors, it's worth it.

Chapter 10
Communicating Bad or Difficult News

No business, however large, however small, is immune to downturns and difficulties. Revenues can fluctuate; staffing needs and required work hours can decrease. Sadly, there are other kinds of events that must be communicated to employees, stakeholders, and other interested parties, such as the departure, illness, or death of a coworker or the closure of the business.

As the owner/operator of the business, it's your responsibility to communicate difficult or bad news to the people involved in your business.

Announcing Salary Freezes or Cuts

Despite your best planning, your business may suffer periods of lower sales, revenue, and profit such that it can survive only if employees are willing to accept a salary freeze or cut, either temporarily or permanently. Here are some phrases to help you discuss this issue, either one-to-one or at a staff meeting.

- Unless we do something now, this business will have to close within three months. I'm personally taking a 50 percent cut in salary, and I need you to agree to a 20 percent reduction for three months. I know this hurts, and of course I will understand if you prefer to look for employment elsewhere.

- I appreciate your hard work this year. Unfortunately, our market took a nosedive, and I cannot give you the raise that you certainly deserve.

- I have had a tough choice to make. Rather than lose any of my employees, I have opted for cutting back on wage increases temporarily.

- Regretfully, until business improves, the only way to avoid layoffs is to roll back our salaries two years.

- Because of the recent slowdown in our marketplace, I regret to tell you that I have to cut your hours by half. I wish I could continue paying you in full in spite of this cutback, but I cannot. This measure is only for the short term. I look forward to returning to full time soon.

- Please understand that cutting back all of our salaries is a temporary measure that will help us survive and ensure our future success as employees and as a company.

■ The majority of our bread-and-butter clients are experiencing tough economic setbacks. Their problems affect our company's bottom line. So until those clients can resume business with us, we will have to cut our work hours by 25 percent, which unfortunately means a 25 percent reduction in salaries.

■ This is a tough announcement for you to hear and for me to make. You consistently give me 150 percent of your efforts, but during this current market depression I am unable to reward you with the bonuses you so deserve. With a little patience, we'll all get through this tough time.

Requesting More Work Hours

Particularly in small businesses, there will be times when there's a need for people to work more hours for at least a short time. In retail, employees tend to work longer hours to accommodate the needs of customers and to maximize revenues. In project-based businesses, deadlines can require intense work. Keep in mind that in some situations, more hours can mean more money, so it's not always bad news for employees.

Here are some phrases that you can use to request or require that employees increase their work hours.

■ This huge order will make our reputation. So we can meet our customer's delivery schedule, we are asking that everyone work an extra day per week for the next three weeks. This is a temporary investment of time that will yield a good return, and we'll compensate all of you with overtime pay for the extra hours and a generous bonus when we beat the deadline.

■ I am asking you for more hours at the same pay. I understand some of you can't do that or don't feel comfortable with it. That's fine. It's up to you. But for those who choose to stay, here's the bonus plan I'm putting in place, so if we hit our targets you'll make much more money.

■ You are an asset to my company. I would like to have you go from part time to full time. Your hourly rate will remain the same, but we will review it after six months.

■ Since the flood this spring reduced all of our work hours, we need to make up lost time so we can fulfill customer orders. This mandatory overtime may place a burden on your family with regard to childcare; we can help. Please approach me individually about this issue and any other family issue you may be concerned about.

- In order for our shop to take advantage of the tourist season, we will expand our hours of operation to seven days a week with extended evening hours. Before I make a formal request for extra hours, I would like you to decide as a group how you will cover the extended hours. Overtime rates will apply on Sunday and extended evening hours.

- I appreciate that having to work more hours upsets your work-life balance. When this crunch is over, I will ensure that you all have the opportunity to make up the family time you've missed.

- You'll notice that I'm going to be coming in at 7 a.m. and staying until 8 p.m., six days a week, until we are all caught up. I hope you'll all pitch in with me on this.

Announcing Job Description Changes and Duty Changes

One of the advantages of small businesses over huge companies is that they can change direction much more quickly and change employee tasks and assignments almost instantly, particularly when the owners and managers maintain a good relationship with each employee.

There will be times when your business needs dictate that one or more employees take on new job responsibilities and tasks or drop some that are no longer needed. Some employees may be pleased with these changes, while others may see them as negative. You still need to know how to effectively communicate changes in job duties. Here are some phrases to guide you.

- Over the last year our business has changed a lot, so I'd like us to get together, since we're a small group, and see if there is a better way to allocate job responsibilities. I'm hoping each of you will be happier by having input on your job tasks.

- Now that we have automated our inventory system, your duties will include keeping current with changes to the system provided by our software vendor and sharing them with our users. This new opportunity will get you ready for future challenges I have in mind for you.

- I know you've been having a tough time with your work lately. Who can blame you, with all the stress at home? That's why I am hoping you agree to be temporarily assigned to work with Barb until you and I decide that you're ready to work out front again.

- In order to use your talents and skills more effectively, I have decided to change everyone's duties and responsibilities. If any of you foresee any problems, please speak with me.
- Up to now, Jackie has been responsible for following up with customers. Now she's going to be doing some design work, so we need someone else to do customer follow-ups. I'd like to know if anyone wants to volunteer for the task.
- I have been comparing the work you're doing now with your job description. It seems that you are outperforming your job description! You deserve a raise. And one of your first tasks will be to update your job description.
- In order to serve our Spanish customers better, we'll be promoting bilingualism here. I'd like at least half of you to attend training in Spanish. If you can master the language, you'll receive a raise, since you'll be more valuable. Of course, we'll pay for the training and offer time off to attend. Who's interested?
- Since nobody has volunteered for Spanish language training, we have only one choice. We're going to make Spanish a job requirement, at least for counter staff. In the next year you can take advantage of our offer to help you learn, or it's possible that we'll have to let you go and hire others who can serve our Spanish clients.

Reporting Government Regulation Changes

Some industries and businesses are quite heavily regulated and/or influenced by government regulations. For example, restaurants and food-related businesses have to abide by very strict codes for food safety. Businesses of a certain size may have to abide by workplace, safety, and health regulations as well as laws requiring accommodations for people with disabilities. In addition, if you do business with government agencies, you will find that there are frequent changes in the requirements for such business relationships.

Here are a few phrases to use with your employees when changes in government regulations create challenges for you and your employees.

- The government is cracking down on the food industry, so I'm going to remind you that you must follow the hand-washing rules posted at each food preparation station. Since we could be closed down if we're caught violating those rules, I'm prepared to fire any employee who does not follow the posted rules.

- I've just received the new requirements for making proposals and bids to the government. As usual, it's going to get harder to get government business. I'd like all of you to read the document and come up with some suggestions as to how we can abide by the rules and get more contracts.

- The new anti-smoking regulations forbid smoking within 50 yards of office building entrances, so I'm afraid we have to ask you not to smoke adjacent to the building. None of us wants the company to gain a bad reputation or get hit with fines. I can recommend smoking at …

- The county health inspectors have put out a warning about the quality of the drinking water in this area, so do not drink any tap water and, even more important, do not let customers drink our tap water. Direct them to the cooler we've just installed, and make sure that the signs we're posting at the water faucets and fountains remain in place.

Canceling or Altering Vacations

Sometimes it's necessary to change a few scheduled vacation times to address a particular business need. In extreme cases it may be necessary to ask all your employees to modify their plans. If that need arises, here are a few phrases to use.

- I know that changing vacation times is a hassle. I promise you that I too will be postponing my vacation indefinitely, until we've got things stable here.

- I've just learned that our backlog of orders has increased to the point that we need almost all of you to work during July to fill those orders. I know some of you have vacations planned. If any of you who have scheduled time off in July would like to volunteer to work instead, I'll add three days to your vacation allotment. If nobody volunteers, I'll have to cancel all vacations for July.

- We need a skeleton staff between Christmas and the New Year. Right now, most of you have scheduled to take time off that week. If one or two people would like to change their plans and work then, I would greatly appreciate the cooperation.

- Sales and revenue have been down drastically in recent months. Unfortunately, we need to ask for volunteers to take some unpaid time off. This would be an ideal opportunity for those who might like to spend a bit more time with the family or for a trip.

Reporting That the Company Is in Trouble

When your business falters or is experiencing serious challenges, you have to decide when and what to tell employees. Telling them too early may cause your best employees to jump ship, while waiting too long is unfair and tends to encourage rumor mongering.

Regardless of when you share bad news, you need to be as honest as possible about the situation. Here are some phrases to guide you.

- During our last year, revenue has been down significantly. We've had large losses for the last two quarters. We need to take action. I'm counting on all of you to help figure out a strategy to get us back into the black.

- You may know that our revenue is down, but I'd like to reassure you that we aren't going to lay off anyone for the next six months. My goal is to keep all of you, and I promise to keep you all informed.

- You may have heard that because of our financial problems, Jared will no longer be working with us, at least for now. Laying off anyone is hard, and Jared has been a good employee, but we had to make a hard decision. I'm taking Jared to lunch tomorrow, and I'd like to invite you all to attend—I'm paying the tab—to say goodbye and wish him luck.

- I thought it was fair to warn you that if things don't pick up in the next two months, we won't be able to pay our rent. I promise that you'll get all your wages if we close. Also, I understand if you want to start looking for another job.

- I'm sorry to tell you all that as of June 30th we'll be closing our doors. We gave it a good try, but competition has increased, and we simply can't compete with the big chains. I want to thank you all. I will be glad to supply you with positive letters of reference and anything you need to apply for unemployment insurance.

Dealing with Personal Tragedy

Tragedy can strike at any time through accidents, sickness, and the death of employees, relatives, and customers. While it's probably not appropriate to dwell on tragedies when they occur, it is important to acknowledge them. Here are some examples of phrases that show how you can talk about tragic circumstances. Obviously you need to exercise good judgment that takes into account privacy needs and the need to show empathy and support.

- I'm sorry to have to tell you that Jack passed away suddenly on Saturday night. I know all of us had great respect for him. I've talked to his family, and I'll be posting the funeral details soon. Please feel free to take the time away from work to attend. In lieu of flowers, the family would appreciate donations to the Heart Association.

- I've been informed that Tom will be leaving the firm immediately due to health issues. I want to respect Tom's privacy, so if you know any details about his health, please don't share them with others. Thanks.

- To our valued customers: Due to the death of one of our employees, our business will be closed all day on January 7th so we can pay our respects to our fallen colleague. We hope you understand, and we apologize for any inconvenience.

- I know our loss hurts. I've arranged for a grief counselor to be on call if any of you want to talk about it. Or feel free to come talk to me if you feel the need. Here's the phone number of the counselor. You can also talk with her in person here on Tuesday.

Guiding Principles

When bad things happen, employees will often have some idea something is going on, even if you don't tell them officially. If they do not know, but suspect something is going on, that can damage morale and productivity far more than if they know what's happening. Consider this when deciding what to tell employees and when to tell them.

Lead by example. If employees must take a cut in salary, you go first and take an even bigger cut. Employees will help you get through tough times when they know you are suffering and sacrificing too.

The need for privacy and confidentiality often competes with a desire to be open, honest, and timely with bad news. There's no formula to follow, so you have to exercise your best judgment.

Chapter 11
Challenging Customer
Situations

t's inevitable that some interactions with customers will tax your tolerance, patience, comfort levels, and skill. Customers may be darned important for your small business, but they aren't always right, and they aren't always easy to deal with. Even if you don't usually deal directly with clients and customers, you need to be able to teach your employees how you want them to deal with these challenging customer situations.

In this chapter we'll cover phrases to use in challenging customer service situations, from making cold calls (usually difficult for most people) to dealing with unreasonable customers.

Cold Calling

Very few people enjoy cold calling, the process of contacting a customer or potential customer without having been introduced. Most hate cold calling with a passion, which makes it a challenging customer situation. Here are some phrases that can help you.

- I'm calling from [company name] to see if I can increase your Web site traffic in order to get the word out about your excellent services.

- This is Edward from [company name]. I'm contacting you to help make your company a household name.

- I'm from [company name]. Your reputation for business continuity software in the East is exceptional. I would like to discuss the possibility of introducing your product in the West.

- We have just introduced the CalcandPay Software Company out West and think that your company would be the next logical company to be introduced here.

- Is early next week or later in the week a better time to meet with you?

- Learning how to increase your revenues by 75 percent will take the time of a coffee break. Would 2:30 next Wednesday work for you?

- I know that your time is important, and I wouldn't want to meet with you if I didn't think that my information could improve your business.

Difficult Customers

Customers can be difficult in many different, yet frustrating, ways. Their expectations may be unrealistic, or they may try to gain an advantage over you or even steal from you. Or they may feel frustrated themselves. Customers have bad days, too. Regardless, it's possible to retain difficult customers, set guidelines, or even fire difficult customers who are more trouble than they are worth.

In this section we'll offer some generic phrases that can work with difficult customers. Then, in subsequent sections, we'll offer more phrases for more specific situations.

- I know that rules and regulations are hard to take at times. But here's why we need to have proof of your age before we can sign you up.

- It's often tempting to cut corners, isn't it? But I know you'll be happier with the results when you follow each step precisely.

- You seem to prefer the cheapest option. That's understandable, but we don't advise our clients to go that route. You'll spend more time and money in the long run.

- You have tried on every formal gown in our store and not one seems quite right to you. Let's discuss other options for your exciting occasion.

- Your last encounter with a car repair shop sounds extremely frustrating! Here at Autobods, we take the time to discuss all of your repair options with you. We love to help you save money whenever we can.

- I don't blame you for being wary about this kind of business. Let me tell you how we are different, so you don't have to worry about having that kind of experience again.
- I understand your concerns. Let me assure you that our refund policies cover every scenario you have listed.

Dealing with Rude Customers

Customers may be rude because they don't know any better, they are frustrated and taking it out on you, or they are trying to bully and intimidate to gain some advantage. Here are some phrases to use that are assertive and firm, yet supportive. Make sure your employees are properly trained to deal with rude customers. These perfect phrases can help them, too.

- I know you're unhappy with the service. If you would like to speak with my supervisor, let me connect you to her.
- I can see you are dissatisfied. Well, you are talking to the right person, since I'm the owner and will do my best to help.
- I can see you want to have this resolved right away. So let me ask you some questions, and we'll see what we can do to help you.
- Is there another option that we can offer you?
- We want to help you, sir, but before we can start to troubleshoot, we need to know the exact error message you are receiving.
- This type of issue needs our resident expert. He's our best guy and will be happy to help you out.
- I'm willing to stay on the line to help you with your problem, but I am asking you to stop making those comments about my background. If you persist, I'll have to end this conversation.
- I'm assuming that you are less than comfortable dealing with a female mechanic. But no one else is available at the

moment. So the choice is yours. Do you want to get started so I can get your car on the road again?

■ I understand you've been swearing at my employee. I own this business, and I won't tolerate any abuse toward staff or me. I'll help, but you must stop swearing and yelling, or else the conversation will end. OK?

Dealing with Impatient Customers

We all hope for fast service these days, and some of us tend to become impatient even when waiting only short periods of time. Some of us also become impatient when asked to conform to rules and regulations. How you deal with impatient or frustrated customers can make the difference between losing a customer, who will then tell others about his or her unpleasant experience, and keeping an even more loyal long-term customer.

- I apologize. This long delay is unusual, but several of our wait staff called in sick today. I can take your order now.

- Perhaps you didn't notice that this is the beginning of the line. Let me serve the rest of the customers in the line, and then I'll be happy to help you.

- These policies are in place to protect our customers. They may seem a waste of time, but at the end of the day you'll be glad that you followed through with them.

- Sir, I know you want your information now, but there are a few people ahead of you who need their information, too. We want to be as thorough with our other customers as you want us to be with you.

- What sets us apart from our competitors is the care with which we handle your custom order. Your signature here indicates that you were aware when you placed your order that delivery could take a month.

- Let me see what I can do to shorten your wait, maybe by a week or so.

Dealing with the Customer Who Bullies

Not everyone is nice. Some people use bullying tactics to get their way, either intentionally and consciously or without thinking, since bullying tactics have worked for them in the past. You should know that people often use bullying behavior (blustering, yelling, nonverbal intimidation, swearing, etc.) when trying to get something to which they are not entitled.

Regardless of why a customer is aggressive and bullying, as the owner/operator of the business, you are the final arbiter of how to deal with the customer. Even if others are handling most of the direct customer contact, you need to know how to assist them when required.

- Sir, threatening me isn't going to help matters in the least. How about we try to work together on this?
- I will do my best to work on this with you, but I can't do so if you continue your aggressive behavior.
- If you continue to swear at me, I'll have to ask you to leave.
- If you continue to scream at me, I'll have to end this conversation.
- I'm here to help you, but insulting my abilities is slowing down the process. Would you like to deal with another rep, or should we try to resolve your problem?
- I'm sure you want to get right down to business, so maybe we can put aside the personal comments.
- We just need some information, and then we can process your refund immediately. I know that's frustrating, but if you can give me the information, we can finish this up in two minutes.
- Great. I'll get your refund, and you can be on your way.

Firing a Customer

There are times when a particular customer is so demanding or offensive that it's not worth your time and frustration to keep him or her as a customer. In fact, you may not want to do business with the person again. That's your prerogative—provided you are not violating any laws related to discriminatory practices in your jurisdiction.

Before you decide to "fire" a customer, be aware that you must weigh the consequences of further angering that customer. Then, keep in mind that firing a customer should be done with tact, civility, and discretion. That's for your own protection and the health of your business.

- I don't think you and my business are a good fit any longer. It's time to end this association.
- Your needs have changed a lot since we started working together. It seems like a good time for you to step back and consider what it really is that you are looking for.
- You don't seem to respect my employees, and it seems you're not happy with us so far. I think your business needs can be handled elsewhere.
- We have taken our business association as far as we can. Let me recommend other companies that can meet your current needs.
- We have extended you every professional courtesy in allowing you to make your payments late, but I am afraid that we can no longer afford to do business with you.
- It's unfair of us to pursue a business relationship with you. Both of us can do better elsewhere.

Managing a Customer's Expectations

Much customer frustration and anger can be prevented by managing a customer's expectations right from the beginning of the relationship. For example, when you set a completion or delivery date with the customer, you can set it later than when you expect to be able to complete or deliver. This enables you to beat the deadline and provides a cushion in case things go wrong. Managing a customer's expectations helps you keep those expectations realistic and delight the customer by exceeding them.

- Based on what we've talked about so far, I understand your needs. But let me explain why your product choice can only meet 75 percent of your "must-haves."
- I just wanted to let you know that your order is still being processed, and we are expecting to deliver it to you on time.
- Unfortunately, your order has been delayed by a few days. Please accept our apologies.
- Your order came in today, but only half of it has been filled. The rest will be delivered Thursday of next week.
- We normally deliver to customers within two weeks of ordering. We'll notify you of any changes to our delivery schedule.
- Our policy is cash back on returns with no questions asked.
- It takes time to customize a week-long training seminar. I can have a customized training session designed and ready for delivery two weeks after you complete and return the needs assessments that I send to you.

Apologizing to a Customer

Nobody is perfect. Not you. Not your employees. And your business can't be perfect. When mistakes are made that affect a customer, how you deal with the situation makes the difference, once again, between losing the customer and making the customer more loyal. Apologizing when necessary is an important aspect of managing customer relations.

Keep in mind that as boss it's your responsibility to apologize on behalf of your business even if the error was made by an employee. An apology coming from you will be worth tons of good public relations.

- Before we talk about making things right, let me apologize for inconveniencing you.

- It's not fun starting a project, only to find that the kit you are using is missing an essential tool. We will, of course, give you a new kit and provide you with the kit for the second course at no additional cost.

- We are sorry for the delay. While you wait, have a cup of coffee or tea on us. The coffee is a Colombian blend, and we have orange pekoe, green, and oolong teas. We appreciate your patience.

- We didn't anticipate the new bestseller flying off the shelf so early in the day. While we restock, please browse our bargain bin. We can offer you an additional 10 percent discount on the already reduced items.

- My sincere apologies to you and your family for having to put up with such inferior accommodations during your recent trip. We know you work hard and deserve the perfect family vacation.

Making Things Right with a Customer

Apologies are important, but when things go wrong, consider offering something more tangible, particularly if your error has inconvenienced the customer. Offering a bonus over and above what you owe the customer is a good way of creating goodwill when something goes wrong.

- We are sorry to say that we cannot fix your camera. We are prepared to replace it with our latest model. We hope you'll be pleased with your upgrade.

- I'm sorry I have to postpone my course delivery. Hopefully I have given you enough notice. When I can reschedule, I would like to offer your firm an additional course free of charge.

- Please accept our sincere apologies for mixing up your order. I'll make a note of our mistake. The next time you come in, tell us your name, and your order will be free.

- We regret causing you hardship. Please schedule an appointment with us to discuss compensation.

- The flooring material you bought from us appears to be defective. Unfortunately, it must be removed. Because of your lost time and inconvenience, we'll remove the flooring and install the appropriate flooring at no cost to you.

- I take full responsibility for not correctly fixing your plumbing problem yesterday. Your repair is my first priority today. Also, the next time you need us, we won't charge you for our labor, just for parts.

- To show you we value your business, if you book your next family vacation with us, I can offer a 12 percent discount on hotel accommodations.

When the Customer Is Wrong

Customers are not always right. That's reality. How do you deal with a customer who is simply wrong? You need to deal with stubbornly wrong customers with tact and firm gentleness, keeping in mind that the discussion shouldn't be about who "wins" or even who is right or wrong. It should be about finding a solution that suits the both of you and maintains your relationship with the customer.

- Yes, sir, it is our policy to beat our competitors' prices by 15 percent, but we need to see proof of your offer before we can give you a discount.

- Wow! This is one of the toughest frying pans on the market. I've never seen one with a hole almost burned through it. Would you like a replacement or a refund?

- I'm sorry, ma'am. Yes, I can see that the sale sign is still in place. But the sale end date indicates yesterday's date. I have to charge you full price.

- Well, you're right, Madam. The sale sign is still in place, but it shows the sale end date as yesterday. I can still give you the sale price today.

- I can see how you mistook this product as one of ours. The packaging is very similar, isn't it? You'll need to return it to the store where you purchased it.

- I'm willing to refund you the price of the course delivery, since canceling the course was out of your control. However, I think it's a fair compromise for you to compensate me for the traveling expenses I've incurred.

Being the Boss: Dealing with Customers Referred to You by Employees

You can help your employees deal with difficult customers by encouraging them to refer problems to you. Often that can reduce the total time spent resolving issues, since customers tend to respond more positively to those who they feel have more status and power—such as the owner. Here are some phrases to use with customers whom your employees have referred to you.

- Hello, Mrs. White. John, the cashier you spoke to, tells me you're having difficulties assembling your new treadmill.
- I know it's frustrating to have to repeat yourself, but I want to make sure I understand your problem and help you solve it quickly.
- So sorry to have sent you to so many people, Mr. Black. Your situation is a rare one for us, and we want to provide you with our best service.
- Rosanna has asked me to help you, Mrs. Green, because I'm the resident expert with your type of problem. Let's see what we can do to help you.
- Mr. Jones, your problem is more complicated than I can help you with. Let me pass you to someone with the expertise that you need.
- This particular product has caused many problems for our customers. May I connect you to someone who will get some information from you so that we can refund you the full price of your purchase?
- I'm the owner of the business, and the buck stops here, so if there's anything we can do to help, I'm the one to speak to.

Guiding Principles

When you are faced with an abusive or insulting customer, it is absolutely critical that you not respond directly to any insults (especially baiting), that you show empathy and understanding, and that you continue to refocus the customer on solving the particular problem.

That said, you need to be firm about what customer behavior is acceptable, what is unacceptable, and how you expect customers to treat you and your employees.

If you have employees, help them learn how you expect them to handle difficult customer situations and when they can approach you to help out (such as by referring a customer to you). Let them know what they can and cannot do in tough situations.

View problem customer situations as opportunities to win over the customer. How you react to problems or errors can place you above your competitors in the minds of your customers.

Chapter 12
Choosing and Using
Business Premises

For many small businesses, one of the largest regular expenditures goes for business premises. For that reason alone, it's worth considering what kind of premises you want and need, and how your premises and location fit into your marketing strategies.

It may surprise you to consider your premises as linked to marketing strategy, but clearly, where you locate and how you furnish and arrange your business space will affect how your brand is perceived and, in general, how potential customers see your business. It's also clear that the type of business premises you choose will depend on the demands of your business type.

Your business needs determine what you can and cannot do in choosing your business premises. Remember that, and try to let your business needs drive things. Be objective with your decisions, and don't get caught up in the excitement of having a "cool" space. You may be living with that choice for a very long time.

Is a Home Office Right for Your Business?

For the most part, a home office works as a main business location if you are the sole operator (i.e., no employees), if you have one or two employees who can use your home office to carry out their job tasks, or if you have employees who need not work in a single location, but can also work from their homes. Generally, home offices fit situations where any work done with customers or clients happens on their turf, not yours, or when work with customers is done one at a time, so that the business premises need not be accessible to many customers at one time.

Here are some questions you can use to assess the suitability of locating your business in your home.

- Will I have the privacy that I need to run my business?
- Am I isolated enough from others in the house so that they will not interrupt phone conversations or client visits?
- If I need to have clients visit, is there a separate entrance to the office area?
- How will using a home office affect the perceptions of my customers and potential customers?
- Are there significant tax advantages for locating my business at home?
- Will zoning regulations be a problem?
- Is there a potential for neighbors to complain about visitors to my business?
- Do I have enough room to house my office equipment in a home office?
- Do I have room to expand my home office, if need be?
- Will "off-hour" phone calls or faxes disturb my family?

- Will I be distracted from my business by being at home?
- Will I be able to strike a healthy work-life balance in spite of the proximity of my office to my home?
- Does having a home office fit in with my marketing plan?
- Will a home office make it easier or harder for my prospective clients to find me and access my services?
- Will the relative isolation of a home office interfere with my mental health?
- How will I be able to balance being alone in my office with my need for social contacts outside the office?
- Am I disciplined enough to "go to work" in my home office in the same way as I would go to work elsewhere?

THE HOME OFFICE: SPEAKING WITH CUSTOMERS AND FAMILY MEMBERS

Working from home has become more accepted these days. However, there can still be some image problems with a home office, so you need to be able to manage the expectations of customers and use the home office to establish competitive advantage. Further, you need to manage the other people in your home to ensure that you can run your business effectively without causing family problems. Here are some phrases to use to address these two issues.

With your customers:

- One of the reasons I chose to have a home office is so I could play a bigger role in raising my children, since family is important to me.
- The home office eliminates over an hour of commuting every day, and that allows me more time to meet your needs as my client.

- By using a home office, I've eliminated enough overhead to be able to offer you premium service at a price below those of other companies that have to pay thousands each month for their office space.

- Since most of my customers come from the immediate neighborhood, it just made sense to open up the shop in my home, since it's so convenient for my customers.

- Most of my customers, such as you, don't need to be impressed by an expensive location or fancy furniture; what they do want are the skills, knowledge, and benefits I can offer, so I don't try to impress people with fancy exteriors.

With family members and friends:

- When I'm in my office and the door is closed, it means that I shouldn't be interrupted unless there's an emergency.

- You can interrupt me if someone is sick, or has had an accident, or something similar. I'll come out every hour or so, so that'd be the best time to talk to me about nonemergencies.

- Just like you, Daddy needs his space, so this is my room, just like you have your room. That's where I do my job, so I need you not to go in there when Daddy's not there, OK?

- Jackie (friend), I know you have my work number, but I'd appreciate it if you use my home number for personal calls. Usually you'll get voice mail, but I check for messages every few hours, and I'll get back to you.

- John (friend), I know it's easy to drop in on me since you know I'm always "home," but I need to make a living, and unexpected interruptions can interfere with my work, or worse, be embarrassing if I have a customer here. If you want to see me during work hours, please call and we can set a time.

Buying Your Business Space

Owning a separate business premises adds a considerable level of complexity to running a small business. If you're starting up, you should consider carefully whether purchasing your space is wise or whether you should delay until you have succeeded in rented premises. Here are some questions to consider.

- Am I prepared to make a commitment to maintaining the property and be solely responsible for upkeep?
- Is this property up to code with current building standards?
- Is the property zoned properly for my business?
- What renovations are required to turn this property into my business space?
- Is this a suitable location for my business? (See below, "Choosing Your Location.")
- What plans, if any, are being made to revitalize the part of town in which this property is located?
- Do the neighboring business owners plan to remain in their present locations?
- Am I prepared to take on the responsibility of a mortgage?
- How easily could I resell this property at a profit?
- What are the tax advantages and tax disadvantages of buying business premises?
- Can I live with the inflexibility of anchoring my business in a building I own? Will that limit my options to respond to market changes?

Renting Your Business Space

For many business types, renting space is the only practical option, since many businesses lack the capital or credit to build or own and their businesses do not fit into a home-based environment. Here are some things to consider about renting.

- How often will the rent be reviewed and possibly raised?
- Is renting my business space cost-effective?
- Am I prepared to enter into a long-term rental agreement?
- Is a rental deposit required?
- What happens if I wish to leave prior to the end of my lease?
- Can I sublease this space?
- Are utilities included in the rent?
- If I am responsible for paying for utilities, how can I estimate the cost per month?
- Is the landlord willing to share the costs of building out this property to suit my business?
- Is this a suitable location for my business? (See below, "Choosing Your Location.")
- Is a cleaning service for the office/premises included in the rental agreement?
- What are the tax implications of renting?
- How much space will I have to rent?
- Is the cost per square foot justified by location and customer volume?
- Is there guaranteed exclusivity for my business type in this location (for example, in a mall)?
- Do my target customers frequent this location?

Renting Occasional Business Space

There are companies that provide secretarial services, office equipment, and meeting space to businesses that require these on an occasional or ongoing basis. Renting space occasionally can provide a very professional high-end look for your business when you meet with clients. Similarly, renting secretarial services can help provide a more personalized and professional interaction with customers contacting you via telephone. Such companies offer a range of services, so you may choose, for example, to have a receptionist answer your phones, but not make use of other possible options. Here are some questions to determine if you would benefit from renting space as needed.

- How often will I need such a space?
- Is it likely that I can set up most client meetings to occur at the clients' premises, so I don't need public office space?
- Does it make sense financially to rent occasionally?
- How many renting options are there? Pay per use? Rent by the month?
- Will I make use of most of the office equipment available?
- What accommodations are available for meeting with clients (e.g., refreshments, receptionist)?
- Do the facilities reflect the image that I am trying to project to customers?
- Is the rental cost tied to the type of equipment I use (such as conference phones or faxes)?
- How will my clients perceive this type of meeting place?
- Am I comfortable with implying that the facilities I use belong to me?

- What amenities (such as coffee, water, sodas, or muffins) are included in the rent?
- Is the location convenient to my regular place of business, so meeting with clients does not require much travel time?
- Is parking readily available? Is it free to clients?
- Is the location readily accessible to clients in the market segments I'm trying to reach?

Choosing Your Location

No doubt you've heard that the secret of business success is "location, location, location." While that's a bit exaggerated, it's particularly true for business in the retail and hospitality sectors and certain personal services businesses.

There are basically two parts to the location equation. How easy is it for people in your target market segments to access your location? How easy is it for you to carry out your business tasks? For example, if you regularly mail products to customers, it's much more efficient to be close to a post office than 40 miles away, and if you often need to go out to a copy shop for mass photocopying, it's more convenient if that trip is short and fast.

Still, your major main focus needs to be on your customers. Here are some things to consider.

- Can my customers find my location easily?
- Does the location appeal to the demographics I need?
- Is the location attractive to my customers?
- Is there plenty of foot traffic?
- How easy is the commute for my employees?
- Is there convenient and reasonably priced customer parking?
- Is the location in an area with other prosperous businesses and retail stores?
- Is the location in a low-crime area?
- Do the other businesses in the area complement my business products or services?
- Are there any competitors close by?

- Will the owner guarantee exclusivity for my type of business in the building?
- Is there employee parking?
- Is the location close to business services I need to access on a regular basis?
- Is the location accessible for people with physical disabilities?
- Does the location project the image I have specified in my marketing plan?
- How much space is available if I require space to grow in the future?
- Would I be eligible for any government incentives to locate in a particular area?
- What waste disposal options are available to meet my needs?
- Does the location provide sufficient infrastructure (electricity, plumbing, Internet access, etc.) to fit my type of business?

Outfitting Your Office

Most businesses require an area for paperwork and phone calls; some businesses are entirely office-based. Here are some questions to ask about outfitting your office space.

- How can I ensure that my office projects the right image for my business? (For example, a fine arts dealer may require something different from a law office.)
- How can I make sure my office decor reflects my business?
- Are the office artwork and decor appropriate for my business?
- Is the business space arrangement easy to keep organized and tidy?
- Can I make coffee and water available for clients?
- How can I make the reception area or waiting area inviting to clients?
- If the receptionist is absent, can I hear visitors enter the waiting area?
- Do I want partitions or an open feeling in my office area? (Consider noise, privacy, and ease of communication among employees.)
- Do I want self-contained offices or cubicles? (Consider noise and privacy.)
- What kinds of computer equipment, Internet access, and network do I require?
- Can I purchase last year's technology, or do I require the most recent technology?
- Whom do I need to install and maintain my technologies?
- How can I protect my premises and property (burglar alarm types, security service)?

- How can I lay out my office to ensure confidentiality and security of client and business records?
- How can I lay out my office so that clients do not run into each other or overhear each other, if privacy is critical?
- Is the lighting warm, inviting, and cost-effective? If not, how can I make the lighting more appropriate to my needs?
- What amenities might I need to make my clients comfortable when they visit (e.g., large coffee maker, refrigerated beverages, microwave)?

Guiding Principles

Whatever your type of business, your premises should reflect the image you have identified as advantageous in your marketing strategy. It must attract those in the market segments your business relies on for revenue.

It may be tempting to go wild with your premises, particularly if you have a high line of credit or a lot of cash, but moderation is the order of the day, particularly if you're just starting. Even if you can spend large amounts of money on premises, remember to evaluate each expenditure in relation to its business necessity and potential return.

With the advent of the Internet and related technologies, a lot of business traditionally conducted face-to-face can now be conducted virtually. That means you may be able to have more modest premises by taking advantage of technological capabilities. For example, online meetings can replace regular meetings, eliminating the need for large meeting rooms.

Making choices about business premises almost always involves trade-offs, since each choice you make has benefits and disadvantages. Do your research, and keep your thinking as objective as possible. Avoid being overwhelmed by the excitement of having the coolest place or the fastest computers—unless, of course, there are business advantages.

Chapter 13
The Marketing Plan and
Marketing Strategy

There are many definitions for "marketing." We take the position that marketing is about arranging your business practices so that:

- You meet customer needs.
- Customers are aware that you meet their needs.
- Customers are motivated to purchase from you.
- Customers are motivated to continue to buy from you.

That's a simple approach, at least on the surface of it; below the surface lies much complexity and detail.

Your marketing plan or marketing strategy maps out the information you need to meet these four criteria, plus the actions and budget you will need to make it happen.

As with a business plan, marketing plans can range from very simple, short documents for your own use to extensive documents designed to be part of a business plan you might present to investors. We're going to focus on developing a plan or strategy that you will use to guide your marketing initiatives. In other words, what we describe here is how to plan your marketing actions. In the next chapter, we'll discuss specific methods for communicating with customers and getting your marketing messages out there. If you are doing a formal marketing plan, we recommend finding additional resources to augment what is included in this chapter.

What is the point of investing as much time as possible into creating a marketing plan or strategy? Apart from the need for investors and bankers to have confidence in your marketing abilities, you need to think about marketing and develop a concrete marketing plan to use as a guide. Marketing should involve coordination of a range of methods that reinforce each other; to make that work requires organization. Further, you need to decide how to allocate money and other resources to your marketing efforts. Without marketing, you will have no business. Poor marketers go out of business.

Critical Marketing Questions

Marketing can involve huge amounts of research and analysis, which is beyond the scope of most small businesses. However, developing marketing strategies need not be overwhelmingly complex, since marketing can be simplified to a number of straightforward questions. Think about these questions and answer them accurately and completely, and you are well on your way to marketing your business successfully.

- Who are my customers?
- What do current and potential customers want?
- What motivates or excites my customers (e.g., low price, quality, durability, convenience)?
- What do I want potential customers to know about my business?
- Where do my potential customers tend to get their information (e.g., Internet, radio, newspapers, word of mouth)?
- How do I get their attention?
- Based on my answers to the above questions, where do I need to promote my business to reach my target customers?
- How can I make it easy to buy from us?
- What image do I want to project about the company (e.g., high class, chic, bargain basement, formal)?

Identifying and Understanding Your Customers

While planning to start up and regularly throughout the life of your business, you need to identify (or retarget) your customers (your market segments) and learn enough about them to customize your business to meet their needs and communicate with them. Here are questions to ask members of your market segments, whether current customers or potential customers. You should also add your own questions relevant to your type of business.

- What's the most important thing you look for in a [insert type of business]?
- When you deal with [insert type of business], what's the thing that drives you nuts so you don't want to go back?
- How could we make buying a [insert item] easier?
- Where do you get most of your information about [insert product or service]?
- What drives you nuts about your job (if working business to business)?
- What causes you to trust a [insert type of business]?
- What could we do to provide you with better service?
- What additional services/products would you like us to provide?
- Have you been treated well by our staff?
- What's the worst customer service experience you've had with [insert type of business]?
- What's the best customer service experience you can remember?

- If we have special offers, would you prefer to hear about them by phone, by mail, by e-mail, on our Web site, or not at all?
- Do you visit our Web site?
- When you shop for [insert products or services], where do you tend to go in the city?
- What's most important, price or convenience?

Summarizing Your Customer Characteristics

Once you have information from your current or potential customers, it's worth organizing it into a concise set of statements that describe your market, statements that you will use later to determine specifics about your marketing actions and strategies. Here are phrases you can customize to use in your summary.

- Our main customer group is between 18 and 24, living in [geographic area]. Characteristics of this group include:
  - Substantial discretionary money
  - Desire to be current
  - Want to be different but without being too different
  - Love technology
  - Enjoy online interactions with peers
  - Do 40 percent of shopping online
  - Value informality in both dress and conversation
- Our main customer group is between 45 and 60, male and female, regardless of current geographic location. Characteristics of this group include:
  - Preference for reading things on paper rather than online
  - Prefer personalized service involving a person
  - Mistrust technology or are frightened by it
  - Large discretionary funds
  - Make two to three large purchases a year
  - Prefer simplicity in purchasing
  - Mostly have considerable amounts of leisure time
  - Value well-dressed people and more formal conversation

■ Our main customers are large corporations, and the main decision makers we will deal with are executives, human resource professionals, and senior managers.
Characteristics of this group include:
- Value professionalism at all times, in appearance, grooming, and conduct
- Have exceedingly little spare time
- Hate high-pressure sales tactics
- Want the information and what's in it for them, quickly and concisely
- Demand short written summaries before or after meetings
- Often delegate meetings to junior staff
- Occasionally get swayed by management fads or trends
- Tend to be cautious about making any changes in their purchasing practices or the vendors they use

Considering the Competition

Customers usually look at what is available in the market-place and choose from among the competitors. For this reason, you need to identify how to stand out among the competitors and define your unique selling proposition, or to use another phrase, your competitive edge. To do that, you need to understand your competitors in your market segment.

Here are some questions to answer. In some cases, you can't ask your competitors directly; in other cases, you may actually be able to talk directly with competitors if you work in a collegial field where the demand is healthy.

- How are my potential customers dissatisfied with how their needs are being met by the competitors?
- On what basis are competitors trying to compete (e.g., price, speed of delivery, customization)?
- Are their any weaknesses in the business models of my competitors?
- In what areas can I do things better than my competitors, and how can I use that advantage to better meet customer needs?
- Can I compete on price?
- Are competitors underserving any demographic that might be interested in my products or services?
- Do my competitors have good reputations?
- Is it likely I can take market share from competitors, or is it more likely I can expand the market?

Defining Your Competitive Advantages

It's absolutely critical to define for yourself how you will better fill the needs of your customers. After all, if you can't do that, how will your customers be able to choose to do business with you? Consider your skills and abilities, your experience, and anything else that differentiates your company from others. Create your marketing messages based on the unique value you offer to the customer. Here are some example phrases.

- Since we don't pay high rents, we can offer our services at a lower price than our competitors.
- Due to my skills and experience in a range of business areas, I can provide one-stop consulting services for other businesses related to human resources, something most competitors cannot do.
- We are willing to establish long-term relationships with our customers, even if it costs us a little in profit.
- We are the only [insert business type] within 25 miles of the town.
- We adapt more quickly and develop new products to meet the quickly evolving needs of our customers.
- Our competitors are boring stick-in-the-muds. We are fun and offer an informal, enjoyable experience.

Adapting Your Business to a Changing Marketplace

The information you have about your market, demographics, and competitors should trigger a regular review of your overall business strategy. You may not have thought that marketing includes making changes in your core business if and when you find the market demands such changes. This may mean altering prices, discontinuing products, developing new services, and so on. The adaptation process should be continuous, since those businesses that do not respond to market conditions fail. Here are some questions to help you plan ways to adapt to changes.

- My major competitor is offering a new service that is taking our customers away. How can I counter their move?

- The neighborhood is going upscale. What do I need to do to appeal to the new demographic in the area?

- More people have gotten rid of their large vehicles and bought smaller cars. What can I offer to people who own small cars to make us the business they prefer?

- The large companies we serve are downsizing their employees. Perhaps we can provide new services to accommodate the companies that need to outsource in [insert specialty].

- With layoffs so common, is there room to provide new job counseling services to our corporate clients?

- What's changed in our marketplace during the last six months, and where do the opportunities lie?

- What's likely to change in the next year, and how can we be ready to take advantage of new opportunities?

Pricing Strategy

Price and where you place yourself relative to your competitors are part of the marketing equation. You can determine pricing in various ways, but it's useful to develop a strategy that specifies where you want to be in the market regarding the prices of your goods and services. Here are some phrases to adapt to your situation. Note the emphasis on tying pricing decisions into your market segment and what you know about your target customers.

- Since our customers indicate that price is not a major determinant in choosing where to shop, we see our pricing as being in the middle to high end in the market, so that we can provide extra value-added services for free.

- Our customers have relatively low incomes and will sacrifice service and convenience for low prices. We'll go the no-frills route and compete on price.

- We'll use a mixed pricing strategy, pricing some of our products/services below the going market prices and some of our products/services in the high end for customers willing to spend more money.

Distribution Strategy

If you produce or resell products, either tangible or intangible (such as electronic books and music files), you need to decide on the methods of distribution. In other words, where will customers be able to purchase your products? Here are a few phrases relevant to distribution. Once again, notice that distribution is often keyed to what you know about your customers.

- People in our market segment prefer to buy things online, so we will distribute our products through online vendors (Amazon, eBay), and by doing so, we can reach customers around the world.

- Our pricing strategy dictates that we sell direct to consumers, thus enabling us to keep our prices lower than our competitors' and also creating a sense of exclusivity.

- We prefer to rely on distributors to deliver our products to retailers, since our customers are used to buying [insert type of product] through major retailers.

- Distribution will be limited, to create a brand image that our products are rare and valuable.

Branding and Brand Identity

What do you want people to think about when the name of your company is mentioned or when they think about you and what you offer? What people associate with your brand is a result of marketing. You want your brand to be recognized in your market segment. If you sell widgets and someone needs to buy one, you want your company name to pop into the person's head.

Brand awareness and brand identity and associations do not happen naturally; you need to address them specifically in producing all of your marketing materials, and they may affect your choice of marketing methods. Before you can do that, you need to envision what you want your company name to convey. Here are some phrases you can adapt to use in expressing the associations you want your customers to make about your company brand.

- We will project an image of complete and consistent professionalism in what we do and how we promote ourselves.
- The name [company name] should be synonymous with integrity.
- Our customers will see us as having lower prices but still providing quality services.
- When people think of [company name], we want them to think about champagne and rich chocolate.
- Our name should mean one-stop shopping in the home renovation field.
- We want our restaurant to be seen as the place where families can come and eat healthy food.

Guiding Principles

Marketing involves understanding the needs of your customers, meeting those needs, and communicating the benefits you have to offer in ways that reach your market. This is all predicated on an understanding of your target customers, potential and current.

Marketing is so critical to any business that it's worth learning as much as you can through reading books and attending seminars or college courses. There is so much to it that you can study for years, yet only scratch the surface.

Plan, budget for, and write an action plan to implement your marketing plan. Do this in an organized and systematic way, commit to your marketing plan, and execute. Do not allow other tasks to interfere with your marketing efforts.

Your unique selling proposition should be at the core of your marketing actions. Identify what you do best that your competitors cannot or do not do, translate that into benefits for your customers, and get that message out.

Chapter 14
Marketing Methods

I f you've invested in creating a detailed marketing plan and strategy, you'll have a good grasp of the best ways to get in touch and keep in touch with your customers. For example, you may determine that the demographics of your prospective customers make them more open to shopping on Web sites. Perhaps your desired market segment is fairly conservative and respects well-crafted, "slick" brochures. It may even be that your target customers like high-pressure marketing.

Whatever your situation, you have to execute well. You must create the materials so they work, regardless of the marketing methods and channels you have determined are optimal.

Before we consider some of your marketing options, here's a tip. You may think you know what marketing techniques will work. However, to succeed you'll need to track which marketing methods and channels work for your business and which do not. You should figure out your return on investment and test different methods.

All Marketing Materials

Most effective marketing materials and methods are based on the same principles. Here are the questions you need to ask and answer for all your marketing efforts.

- Is the method or material likely to grab the customer's attention?
- Will the attention be positive and support a positive image or brand?
- Does the material or method explain how the customer will benefit?
- Does the material or method prominently feature how we are different and better (unique sales proposition)?
- Does the material or method provide easy-to-understand ways to purchase our products and/or services?
- Does the material or method create confidence in our company and the brand and create the image I desire?

The Call to Action

A call to action consists of phrases that encourage the customer to do something specific. It can be as simple as "Buy Now," or it can be more elaborate, providing an explanation, such as "act today because quantities are limited." Calls to action are basic to almost all sales and marketing efforts, whether you want the consumer to buy a product or service, contact you for more information, provide information, or sign up for something.

Here's one very important point. Calls to action vary from "high-pressure, high-volume" phrases such as used in infomercials or highlighted and repeated in brochures or on Web sites, to much more subtle (and professional) methods. When in doubt, be conservative with your calls to action, and make sure they reflect your business image. A professional, conservative business requires subtle calls for action. Here are some questions to ask.

- Does my call to action convey a sense of urgency?
- Does it reflect the image I want to project to customers?
- Does it indicate what to do and the benefit of doing so?
- Is my call to action clearly in sight as the person reads the material?
- Is its meaning clear and obvious?

Now, here are examples of calls to action that might be included in any kind of marketing or sales material.

- Click here to become a better manager.
- Click here to register for your free report on …

- Call 555-1212 right now for more information on our special bonus.
- Call now. Only available exclusively from us.
- Order within the next hour and receive a 10 percent discount.
- Order now while supplies last.
- Contact our consultants, who will help design a custom solution for you.
- Call today for your free initial consultation—no strings attached.
- Want to know more about us? Call us at 555-1212.

Web Sites

Web sites are almost mandatory for any small business. If you don't have one, customers will wonder about the credibility of your company. A Web site can range from the extremely basic (a few pages—an online business card) to a large site with thousands of pages, with a full product catalog and a means of buying online.

As with the creation of other kinds of marketing materials, the process can be simple or complex. We'll focus on the kinds of material you probably should have for a generic business site and a few elements that make business Web sites successful.

- Are the colors selected pleasing and consistent with the image I desire? Have I tested the site's navigation? Is it easy to use? Is it easy for visitors to find what they want?
- Do I have the right number of "call to action" phrases? Are they worded appropriately?
- Is there adequate "white space," or does my site seem cluttered?
- Have I kept each page to a reasonable length, so visitors don't have to scroll much?
- Have I considered all types of browsers in my design (e.g., Firefox/Mozilla, Internet Explorer, Netscape, Opera, Safari), so that the site will work for most if not all visitors?
- Have I included a biography of myself that conveys what is special about me?
- Is my contact information displayed prominently?

- Have I included articles or other free material I have created that help prospective clients understand who I am and how I can help?
- Is it easy for visitors to instantly see what the site has to offer?
- Is the ordering process (if selling products) easy to use?
- Does the ordering process provide a sense of security to customers?
- Does the entire site convey the feeling that my company is reputable and trustworthy?
- How can customers get help if the order process hits a snag? Is it clear to them what to do if there is a problem?
- Have I had other people review the site to give me feedback, and have I acted on it?
- Would I want to visit this site? Would I find a reason to return?
- Can I succinctly state what value this site has for customers and prospective customers so they will bookmark it and return to it?

Press Releases

A press release is an announcement that you create and distribute in order to attract media attention to your company's news, new services, or new products. You hope that your press release will cause the media to provide you with free publicity by reviewing your products or services or interviewing you. Attract their attention, and the media will help you market.

Press releases can be targeted to all media types—radio, television, Internet, newspapers, trade journals. Here are some principles.

- Does your press release convey the proper image?
- Have you targeted the release to media who have an interest in the topic, rather than using a shotgun approach?
- Are you treating your press release as a news release, focusing on something new that your company is doing?
- Does it convey enough information to attract media attention?
- Does it focus on what's unusual, beneficial, or novel in what you are doing?
- Does it convey the unique opportunities that your business offers?
- Does it include your business contact information, at least your telephone number and Web address?
- Does your press release avoid high-pressure hype and focus instead on the value of the information in the release?
- Have you written the press release to appeal to the media?

- Have you written the release in the third person?
- Is the press release on your official business letterhead?
- Is the phrase "press release" at the top of the page in bold capitals?
- Have you included a large headline at the top?
- Have you included a release date (either "for immediate release" or "for release July 3, 2009")?
- Have you included who, what, when, where, and why?
- Have you avoided anything that makes your press release sound like a sales pitch?
- Does it contain a human interest angle?
- Does it help members of the media do a better job?

Marketing Brochures and Other Printed Materials

No matter what kind of business you run, you will use printed materials to promote and market your business. Anything that contains information about your business—business cards, brochures, sales flyers, letterhead, and even invoices and receipts—should be considered marketing materials. They are used directly with potential customers as in direct mailings, can be made available to current customers to pass on to potential customers, and can even provide information to the media.

These days a lot more of your printed materials can be designed and produced "in house," but there's a major problem. Most small businesses do not have people with the skills to do the job well. It's easy to do it on computers. It's hard to do it well without training. It's better to have someone with design skills.

Here are some phrases to help the designer, whoever that may be, to produce printed materials that will get results. If you decide to do all the work yourself, these phrases will help you consider the key issues.

- We'll want our printed materials to grab the attention of the 18- to 24-year-olds.
- We want brochures, business cards, and letterhead that use the same graphic elements and colors.
- We're a small law firm, and we need to project an elegant and classy image in all our materials.

- We're a small company with a small budget, and our brochures are just for distribution at our checkout, so we need something simple and cost-effective.

- We already have a logo around which we want to base all of our print materials.

- We need our main message (our unique selling proposition) to jump out in the brochure, both on the cover and in the body text inside.

- Since we will use direct mail to distribute our brochure, we need the dimensions and weight to conform to the size the post office requires to qualify for the maximum discount.

- We'll need about 5,000 copies (pieces, sets) each year.

- We think that our brochures will need to be updated and redone once a year as our products and other offerings change.

- Our overall promotional budget is $X, and our budget for printed material, excluding postage, is $Y.

Networking

Business networking is a means of marketing and promoting your business that requires an investment of time, but little if any money. Networking can occur in various ways.

You can join a network (in person or online) that is specifically designed to enable people in business to interact. Chambers of Commerce sometimes offer these. That's more formal networking, since it occurs within a structure. There are also online formal business networks.

Informal networking can happen anywhere or in any way. You can attend professional associations and parties and talk with people. That's networking. It can be very casual. A plumber comes to your house to fix some pipes. You chat. He asks what you do for a living. You tell him you're a real estate agent and give him a card. The next week you get a call from his uncle, who hires you to sell his house. That's networking, too.

Some people suggest you can be fairly forceful and upfront when networking, but we suggest that your networking efforts should be subtle and based on the principle that you want to get to know other people and you'd like other people to get to know and like you. No sales techniques or pitches here. Listen and ask questions. Listen more and talk less. However, remember that self-disclosure and openness help others be open and helpful with you. Don't be selfish or self-centered! Here are some phrases to guide you in your networking efforts.

- Hi, John. Good to see you again. How is your consulting business doing these days, given the downturn?

- I'm always looking for more business in training design, so if you happen to come across anything, I'd appreciate it if you'd give me a call. And if I hear of anyone needing any remodeling, I'll do likewise.

- Hi, Mary. Did you get a call from Jack Spratt about contracting for your services? He called me, and since I don't do that kind of work, I referred him to you.

- If you like, Jerry, I'd be glad to take some of your brochures and cards and display them on my store counter, if you'd be willing to do the same with my cards and brochures.

- You know, Jenny, it occurs to me that we offer completely different products and services to exactly the same people. Do you think we can work together to market what we offer and share the costs?

- I'm glad to hear about your new agency. If I can offer any help, please give me a call. Here's my card.

- It's been a long time. What's new and exciting with your wife, Cathy, and your two kids?

- If I were to refer someone to you, who would be your perfect customer?

Freebies: Promotional Items, Free Samples, and Free Services

Freebies are either physical items given to potential and current customers or work done at no charge for a business, charitable, or professional organization. You can also offer a free service to bring people to your location.

The physical items you give away can include pens, bookmarks, and similar kinds of promotional items imprinted with your logo and contact information. But it's far more powerful if you can provide free samples of the things you sell. People lose or throw out pens and bookmarks, but if you provide a free sample that has value for customers or prospective customers, they will keep it and remember you.

Consider speaking at a local professional conference for free, if you have the skills. If not, volunteer at events that potential customers might attend.

Here are some phrases to consider using when you're using freebies to promote your company.

- I'd be glad to send you a free sample of our new widget if you would like to give me your business card.
- Get a free manicure just for coming to our salon and joining our mailing list.
- I'd certainly be willing to volunteer to work the desk at the upcoming human resources conference or help out some other way.
- Would you like to take one of our imprinted bookmarks, sir?

- I'd be glad to meet with you for a half hour to discuss your needs—at no cost and at your convenience.
- I'll be glad to talk to you about your problem at no charge. Then, if we like each other, perhaps we can do some business.

Elevator Speeches

Part of networking involves getting across your message in a short period of time and in a way that interests the other person and provides value to him or her. Elevator speeches are short (about 30 seconds) and succinct, usually including:

- Your name
- Unique aspects about what you do
- Benefits for your customers or clients

Elevator speeches are best used in response to a direct question, such as "What do you do?" Foisting an elevator speech on someone who shows no interest is insulting and a waste of time. Here's a sample that could occur at a social event.

- So, what do you do?
- I'm Jock McKean, and I work primarily with governments and charities so less of their money goes toward overhead and more goes toward providing services to taxpayers like you or people in need. Very satisfying work to know I'm helping real people.

If interested, the other person will ask follow-up questions.

Here's another example—an elevator speech made to someone who has asked for summary information about a product to evaluate whether it's worth an investment.

- Our widget is a unique, patented object that can save the average person 20 minutes a day cleaning the house. It's easy to use, and we've sold over 20,000 units in limited distribution.

Media Interviews

Media interviews are exceedingly powerful vehicles for getting the word out about your business. Journalists and producers of radio and television shows are hungry for news items and human interest stories. They tend to be interested in local personalities and businesses, provided they think their listeners and viewers will also be interested.

You can approach editors, reporters, and producers directly, particularly if they are local, and inquire whether they might be interested in doing an on-air interview. Phone contact is probably best, supported by a letter, personally addressed to the producer or on-air talent. Local talk shows are probably the easiest to access for appearances.

Prior to doing an interview, consider and answer these questions.

- Have I heard or watched this show before? (If not, do so.)
- Do I have an idea why they are interviewing me?
- How much time will I have (probably only minutes)?
- What's my key message?
- How will I handle challenging questions?
- How can I make sure there won't be dead air (long silences) while I think?
- What's the audience's interest in me?
- How can I make people want to get in contact with me?
- Have I asked the producer about the procedures for the show? If it's television, have I asked how I can best come across—particularly, how I should dress?
- What image do I want to project about my business or topic?

Guiding Principles

Above all, your marketing methods need to be determined by the nature of your market and target customers and the image you want to create that is consistent with your marketing strategy.

Find out where you can reach your target customers, and choose marketing methods based on that. Marketing in ways that will not reach them or that will not get the reaction you want from them is wasteful.

Don't ignore low- or no-cost marketing and publicity, such as networking, volunteering, and media appearances. A successful media appearance can create huge sales.

Here's a cardinal rule for marketing. Focus on your customers' needs and wants rather than your own. Balance the two. Many a business or personal relationship has been soured because a businessperson focused only on making the sale.

Be interested in others, and be interesting!

Chapter 15
Making the Sales

You may have the best product or service on the planet, but prospective customers need to know about it and be convinced to purchase it. The first step to doing that is how you market your offer, and the second step is selling it effectively. Small businesses, particularly one-person shops, tend to have difficulty with sales and marketing, since many people do not have the skills or inclination to enjoy the sales and marketing process. Yet, without marketing and sales skills, there can be no success.

There are many books that can tell you how to sell, and we can't cover all the possibilities here. We can only suggest that you find sales techniques with which you are comfortable, since the methods you use must seem natural or you will seem suspect or disingenuous to potential customers. We cover marketing issues in other chapters; here you will find phrases to use in sales situations.

Selling a Service

Contrary to what many believe, selling does not involve extolling the virtues of what you have to sell. What it involves is explaining the match between the customer's needs and wants and how what you're selling can satisfy the customer. By necessity, that involves learning about the customer—getting to know him or her, whether you are a corporate trainer, a plumber, or a hairdresser. Here are some phrases for selling a service.

- Can you tell me what kind of training you are you looking for?

- Tell me why you chose training as a method to solve your departmental problems.

- How soon do you want your department staff trained and ready to use the new software?

- Describe for me the typical situations that you hope can be helped by this training?

- Could you explain any constraints (time, budget, resistance) that may exist during the training delivery?

- Describe any issues you need to have specifically addressed during the training.

- Elaborate on the mind-set of most of the training attendees.

- What kind of hair style might you be interested in?

- That's good. We specialize in exactly that kind of cut!

- Here's why the training we offer should be an excellent fit. You said [insert paraphrase], and our training provides [insert characteristics that match].

Selling a Product

As with services, it's important to get information from the customer about his or her wants and needs so you can form a *value proposition* for the customer. The value proposition, described later in this chapter, presents the benefits the client will receive from purchasing what you have to offer.

- What kind of flooring are you looking for?
- Where would you like your new flooring to be installed?
- When do you want your new flooring delivered?
- Why are you thinking about replacing your flooring?
- What kind of instruction manual are you searching for?
- How many copies of the manual do you require?
- Who will be using the manuals?
- Will your new area rug be placed in a high-traffic area?

Overcoming Objections

The mark of a good salesperson is the ability to overcome customer objections. Most customers will hesitate at least a little when purchasing any item of significant cost or even getting back in touch with you. That's normal. A good salesperson can sell to these clients by working through their objections. This can be done ethically and without high-pressure tactics. Below are some examples of phrases that can be used to overcome different kinds of objections.

Objection: "I already have a supplier."

- What is your current supplier not doing for you?
- Are you totally happy with your current service?
- In just a few minutes, I can prove that you will save time and money by switching to our product/service.
- How long has it been since your current supplier has met with you (or asked to meet with you) to discuss the current trends and updates to your product/service?
- How long has it been since you've reviewed your needs with your current supplier?

Objection: "This is more than I'm willing to spend."

- We have a wide range of pricing options. Based on our discussion, your business needs seem pretty basic and would require the least expensive package.
- Well, let's discuss your needs and problems to see if we can work out a more agreeable price range.
- Overall, our prices may seem high, but many of our clients have been able to eliminate some other expenses as a

result of using our products/services. Let me give you a
few examples.

■ The success rates of many of our clients have more than
offset the cost of implementing this solution.

■ Let me talk to you about the many ways in which you can
use this product.

■ Let me spend a few minutes explaining to you the many
benefits of doing business with our company.

■ Doing business with a quality provider/supplier is less
about the money you pay than the quality of the goods
and services you receive.

■ I have some surprising statistics here that prove that your
customers are more concerned with quality and service
than cost.

■ Paying a little more up-front for our quality product/serv-
ice will boost your company's/department's bottom line.
Let me show you how.

■ Can you put a price tag on customer satisfaction and customer loyalty?

■ A small investment now can mean larger profits tomorrow.

**Objection: "I'm happy with my current supplier/provider/
product/service."**

■ Are you certain that your current supplier understands the
changes that your business is currently undergoing? Let
me share my research with you.

■ Are you certain that your current supplier understands the
changes that your business will experience in the near
future? Let me share my research with you. Then you can
decide based on the new information.

- Can your current supplier help you anticipate the growing trends within your industry?

- Does your current supplier have a plan in place to help you to adapt to new trends within your industry?

- Does your current supplier think in terms of being a partner to your success?

- Does your current supplier provide customer incentives that you can pass on to your customers/clients?

- Does your current supplier stay familiar with new technologies that can potentially reduce your costs?

- Are you aware of your current supplier's/provider's best practices methodology?

- The technology has improved so much the last year, and the price has dropped, so that if you buy a new widget, you'll get far more from your purchase.

- The new cell phones contain cameras, music players, Internet access, and more—all for the same price as you paid for your old phone. It's really worth the upgrade.

Value Propositions—Business to Business

The *value proposition* expresses the benefits the buyer will receive from purchasing your product or service or dealing with your company. The customer's perception of the value must be greater than the costs of doing business with you. A unique value proposition is more specific in that it explains what you, specifically, can offer that your competitors cannot. Value propositions must address the rational wants and needs of the prospective buyer, but often need to appeal to more emotional motives (for example, wanting a red car rather than a silver one or liking something because it's "cool" or makes the customer feel younger).

Here are some value proposition phrases as examples to guide you in doing business with other businesses.

- Based on previous discussions, I understand that your peak business times are … And using our product will decrease work hours by 50 percent during such times.

- I know you want your new employees trained and ready to use your equipment within a week of their hire date. Our training methods are designed to meet any type of time-line.

- You've expressed concern about … And here's how our product/service/company handles that type of scenario.

- We pride ourselves on researching future corporate trends and will make it our business to share news of interest to you at all times.

- Based on the training numbers you've provided to me, we can reduce training time by 25 percent and increase task efficiency by 50 percent.

- My research shows that your major competitor holds 32 percent of the current market share; I can show you how to exceed 32 percent.
- Reducing operating costs is one of your major goals, and using our equipment will allow you to save up to 15 percent per year.
- When you need a service maintenance call, we give you our specific arrival time so that you can plan your business day more effectively.
- Our warranty period is double that of our closest competitor—at no extra cost!
- Your purchases today always result in a discount on your future purchases.
- We always pass our manufacturing cost savings on to you, our customer.
- As your financial advisor, I will ensure that you will be financially ready for retirement at 50 with no change in lifestyle.
- Using my service as a Corporate Health Promoter will make your employees healthier, happier, and less stressed, thus increasing your corporate bottom line.
- Buying my customized client management software will earn your company a reputation as number one in customer service.

Value Propositions—Consumers

Individuals vary in the degree to which they make buying decisions based on logic or emotions. Your value proposition should take both into account, even to the point of placing more stress on the emotions than you would with business customers.

- Not only are all our technical people certified, but we'll come to your home to pick up your computer, so there's no need to be inconvenienced by lugging it into a shop across town. And we'll deliver it fully repaired.

- Just imagine how you'll feel wearing a suit that's completely tailored to fit your body, top to bottom. A perfect fit.

- You don't have to be an expert to arrange for fabulous food at a wedding. That's our job. We'll help you decide on a menu to accommodate all your guests—kosher, halal, vegetarian. All it takes is 30 minutes of your time to talk to us.

- Can you see yourself driving that red Mustang? Here, get behind the wheel and feel it.

- I've helped over 2,000 people organize their wills and enjoy the peace of mind of knowing that their loved ones will be provided for. That's more than anyone else in our town.

- There are hundreds of real estate agents you could use, but only a very few will guarantee the sale of your home. If it doesn't sell within six months, we'll buy it. No need to keep all your plans on hold.

Contacting Former Customers (Retention)

Statistics show that the cost of acquiring a new customer is much higher than the cost of retaining a current one. All businesses, large or small, need to have strategies to retain their customers and keep them happy. This may involve ongoing follow-up and communication, efforts to know your customers more personally, free offers and bonuses, etc. Here are some examples of phrases that you could use with customers who have not done business with you lately.

- When we last met, you spoke of plans to expand your division starting next month. I have some good ideas about your expansion that will allow you to take advantage of today's market.
- I know that you are an avid collector of ... We have just received several of the latest collection. How many should I put aside for your consideration?
- We know that you are searching for ... Today, we learned that we will receive a shipment on Friday. You won't want to miss this opportunity to update your system.
- As one of our valued customers, we just wanted you to know that we've expanded our inventory. So now you can consider us as your number-one supplier of ..., as well as ...
- We've changed our loyalty program. Contact us for more information, and learn how you can save with every purchase.
- If you sign up for our newsletter, you'll receive special coupons that can help you save up to 40 percent on your future purchases. Would you like to do that now?

Rewarding Loyal Customers

Your loyal customers are an excellent investment. They cost little to maintain, and they tend to spread the word about your services and products to others. It's well worth considering how to reward long-term loyal patrons of your business and how to phrase your initiatives.

■ Our unique dining experience can be enjoyed in your neighborhood now. Bring in a friend to dine with you, and we'll comp your desserts.

■ Our company considers you one of our most valued customers. Please fill out this survey to tell us how we're doing, and we'll send you a money-saving coupon to use on your next purchase.

■ Congratulations on the birth of your second son! As your number-one neighborhood sports facility, we invite you to enjoy a first infant swimming lesson for free. Then, if you sign up for the next nine lessons at once, you will receive a 15 percent discount off the regular fee.

■ Here's a "just because you're a great customer" coupon that you can use to get a 40 percent discount on any of our services.

Turning a Browser into a Buyer

In retail, it's common for most people to be browsers and not ready or even interested in making a purchase. This can also occur in service industries, where people may make inquiries to survey the marketplace without intending to purchase. You may be able to turn some browsers into buyers.

Here are some questions that you can use to monitor yourself so you say and do the right things.

- Am I using language that is too technical for the customer?
- Am I providing too much information to the customer at this time?
- Am I giving the customer ample opportunity to ask questions?
- Am I answering the customer's questions clearly?

Here are some phrases you can use with potential customers.

- If you would like to see one of our products demonstrated, don't hesitate to ask for help.
- Just browsing? Take your time; you won't want to miss a thing!
- Just browsing? It's good for the soul.
- Just browsing? Let our products inspire you.
- Just browsing? It's a great day for browsing, isn't it? Have fun. I'm right here if you have any questions.
- We encourage you to comparison shop.

Closing the Sale

The sale isn't completed until the client agrees to purchase and then takes that action. The art of closing a sale can be fairly complex, but here are some phrases to help you wrap up the transaction.

- How soon do you want this new system installed?
- When should I sign you up to receive our monthly newsletter?
- When do you want to start this process?
- Do you want to take your purchase home with you today?
- The next step is for you to ...
- We can prepare your order once you have ...
- We just have the floor model in the store today, but I can have your purchase shipped from another store for you today. May I make the arrangements for you?
- When will you sign the contract?
- How much of a deposit can you leave with us today?
- If you make a commitment today, I'll get the ball rolling on my end, and we can start the process right away.
- I'm looking forward to doing business with you. So what can I do to get this wrapped up for you?

Up-Selling

Up-selling is selling a customer something that is more expensive than what he or she intended to buy. The unethical and shortsighted way to do this is to use high-pressure techniques with a customer. The ethical way is to match the product to the needs and wants of the customer. Often a customer will not be happy with the less expensive product or service because it simply won't satisfy his or her requirements. That's the ideal time to up-sell. When you up-sell to make a customer happy over the long term, you gain a reputation for being honest and credible. Here are some phrases that show how to up-sell.

- Would you like to try another fashion magazine this month? The content is 100 percent Canadian, and all fashions and accessories modeled are guaranteed available in Canadian stores. For $1.50 more, you can enjoy a longer issue every month.
- The sewing machine you are interested in buying will certainly meet your basic expectations, but spending a few dollars more will upgrade you to our next model, which boasts more functions and will ultimately make you happier with your purchase.
- I'm sure that your son will enjoy this mystery novel. You mentioned that he does a lot of cross-country driving for his job. Have you thought about buying the book in audio format? It costs a little more, but it sure would reduce the tedium of all that driving!

- I'm not comfortable selling you this package. You're paying for many features that you've indicated you would never use. Let me show you a different package that, although more costly, will benefit you in the long run.

Cross-Selling

Cross-selling is offering the customer complementary products or services that will enhance the value of his or her purchase. For example, a person who buys a camera might be offered a tripod, some batteries, or other accessories. Here are some examples of cross-selling:

- If you enjoy trying different coffee flavors, why not try this sampler of 10 unique coffee blends and flavors?
- I know you'll be happy with your new bedroom furniture; our linens department has many bed cover sets that will match your new bed-frame style.
- Are you aware that your purchases today just about qualify you to enter this month's contest? If you buy another $15 worth of merchandise, you can earn an entry form.
- You're making a great buy today. To help you take care of your purchase for years to come, consider buying this cleaning kit, formulated to clean, condition, and protect the surface.

Guiding Principles

When trying to determine a customer's needs and wants, use a mix of open-ended questions and closed-ended questions. Open-ended question encourage the person to talk, while closed-ended ones allow you to keep better control over the interaction.

Selling gets a bad rap because many people associate it with high-pressure tactics or other unethical practices. You can sell ethically and comfortably by taking the position that what you have to offer is of real benefit to many people, and that your job is to help link the benefits to the needs and wants of the person.

For a small business retaining customers is critical. Small businesses have limited marketing reach and limited time to market and sell. Pay special attention to your sales and communication tactics, and keep your customers satisfied.

Focus on value propositions and not on product or service features. Features are useless unless they provide value from the customer's point of view. When the customer understands how he or she will benefit, then you'll close the deal.

Chapter 16
Negotiating and
Managing Conflict

I t's simply not possible to avoid conflict if you interact with other people. Even in the absence of conflict, running a small business involves a fair degree of negotiation. You negotiate with suppliers, with customers, and with employees almost daily. Sometimes you negotiate big issues, and sometimes you negotiate things that are so little and commonplace you may not even be aware you are involved in negotiation.

There's both an art and a science to negotiation. We'll start this chapter with some basic phrases that can help you in your negotiating.

Negotiating a Win-Win Agreement

In negotiating (or dealing with conflict) the ultimate goal is not to win and force the other person to lose, but to create a situation where both parties are happy or can live with the outcome. That's because when someone loses in negotiation, there's a tendency for that party to try to get even or harbor anger. That's counterproductive if your goal is to create positive long-term relationships that will benefit your business. In short, it's better to create friends than enemies. Here are some phrases to help you achieve win-win results.

- Let's work at this together until we come up with a solution that we can both live with.
- We need to make sure that we understand each other's point of view fully.
- Let's start by listing the things that we agree on.
- We need to understand what the most important aspects of this issue are to each of us.
- I can compromise and agree on a 7:30 Monday morning delivery, but I need to receive your order by 2:00 Friday afternoons.
- The best scenario is to have your order to us by 12 noon on Fridays, but if necessary we will still do our best to fulfill it even if you can't get it here until 2:00 p.m..
- I value our business relationship and want to find a solution that works for both of us, even if it's not perfect.

Dealing with the Anger of Others

Anger is not always a bad thing, but it can become a serious impediment to fair and rational negotiation, particularly if a person becomes so angry he or she is determined to "win" at all costs. If you negotiate, it's likely you will come across anger in others, so it's a good idea to have some phrases you can use to help calm down the emotional side and encourage rational negotiation techniques.

- I think we're both getting a little tense, so how about if we take a break and resume our talks at about 3 p.m.? Does that work for you?
- It's understandable that you are upset. Let's see what we can do for you.
- Feeling like no one is listening to you can be upsetting; here's how I understand your dilemma . . .
- Oh, well, that's not a good situation for anyone. What can we do to help you?
- I would very much like to help you reach your goals without sacrificing my own, so let's go over the events that got us where you are today and why you might be upset with us.
- I feel that our difference of opinion is making you a little angry. Let's agree to disagree and use this time to totally understand each other's position.
- It may seem like an unsolvable problem for you right at this moment, but I can tell you that you have many options at this point. Let's explore them to make sure you have all the information you need to make your best decision.

Mediating Conflict

There will be situations where it is appropriate for you to intervene in conflicts. Most often this will happen when there are disputes between employees, but conflicts can also occur with business partners and investors. It's probably not a good idea to try to mediate very complex conflicts and disagreements, since advanced mediation requires advanced skills. Here are some phrases you can use in mediating simple conflicts and disagreements.

- Let's determine if there is a real issue here or if we are misunderstanding the situation.
- Let's establish some ground rules acceptable to both of you that we will follow during this discussion.
- One rule to follow during this discussion is absolutely no interruptions!
- Let's ensure that we don't allow little "mini-conferences" to break out around the table. If we are going to resolve this, it will help to be open and transparent.
- We need to define the problem. Sometimes conflicts mask the real problem.
- We need to decide as a group whether this problem is worth resolving. That is, is this problem chronic or a one-time occurrence? Is it just annoying or truly harmful?
- I would like to hear each person describe the problem to make sure that we all understand it.
- As each side explains the problems with the issue at hand, I would also like to hear what each side thinks is working well within the problem area.

- Let me explain that the aim of this mediation session is to first make sure that we all understand the issue from all sides.
- Future mediation sessions will focus on each issue and how we can find a win-win solution.
- John, you've heard Mary explain her perceptions. Before you have your say, could you paraphrase what you heard Mary say?
- Mary, in one sentence could you describe what you want from John, as specifically as possible? Then I'll ask John to do the same.

Staying Focused on Issues

In negotiations and conflict situations, emotions can run high, driving the conversations away from the issues that need to be addressed to resolve the situation or come to agreement. Whether you are an active participant in the conflict or negotiation or a third party helping others to come to agreement, it's useful to have phrases that remind the parties (including yourself) to return to the fundamental issues. It's important to avoid losing focus and going off on tangents, particularly personal and aggressive tangents.

■ I would like to ensure that we all stay focused on the issue at hand during this meeting. With your agreement, I'll interrupt if I feel we are losing direction.

■ As we discuss this issue, other problems may be mentioned that may not be specifically relevant. I would like to reach a group consensus as to whether these problems should be addressed right now or held over for another discussion.

■ I am looking for someone to make a list of all issues mentioned here that will need addressing at some future point.

■ Let's not focus on past conflicts and how they were resolved. Let's just focus on this current conflict of opinions.

■ I know that you've all checked your egos at the door and that you each have an equal interest in resolving this conflict.

■ Let's stay focused on what's at stake here.

■ At the end of the day, I would like to present a united front with regard to our proposed solution to this issue.

- We're both getting emotional here and getting side-tracked. Let's take a break and then come back committed to solving the problem, or at least coming to a conclusion today.
- I'm not going to lose focus and get into personal attacks here, and I would appreciate it if you, also, could stick to the fundamental issue, which is [insert issue].

Stating and Summarizing Problems

Successful negotiation and conflict management both rest on the degree to which all parties understand exactly what problems are at issue. Stating and summarizing problems helps focus the discussions, tends to minimize tangents, and can reduce wasted time.

- The issue is that the reports are delivered late every other week.
- There is a problem with producing monthly reports on time.
- The problem is that my supplier is never available to me when I need to report a shipping error.
- Our current supplier is now delivering inferior products.
- Unknown to the mechanics, our dovetail joint machinery is faulty, causing us to ship defective materials to our customers.
- Joe feels that Gerald is being assigned to all of the tasks that will fast-track his career, while Joe is consistently left with tasks that a junior can easily handle.
- Mary feels that Anne works at a slower pace than Mary, yet still receives rewards for her outstanding output.

Voicing Your Anger and Frustration

We're human beings with feelings that can be ruffled. Sometimes we get angry. The expression of anger and the norms for what is deemed appropriate vary from culture to culture. The prime concern is that however you express angry feelings, you do so in a way that is constructive and doesn't poison the well for further successful negotiation, conflict resolution, and relationship building. There are effective phrasings and damaging phrasings when expressing anger. Also keep in mind that nonverbal factors are particularly important regarding anger, so pay attention to your tone of voice and your body language as well as to your words. All three affect how others will receive your message.

- I feel like no one is listening to me. Please let me voice my opinion.
- This situation makes me angry, but I'd rather not spend time pointing fingers when we could be resolving the problem.
- When you raise your voice and use that tone, I'm not feeling you are treating me appropriately. I suggest we stop now until we've both had some time to cool off.
- The longer this discussion goes around in circles, the more frustrated I'm getting. So let me ask you: Is there a point in continuing this right now, or should we resume at another time?
- At this point I'm so angry at the personal comments that have been made that I'm not even sure I want to continue to do business with you. Where do you want to go with this?

- I am not at all happy that no one has completed the tasks on time. Let's try to deal with the roadblocks and make up for the lost time.
- I am angry right at this moment, but it will fade as soon as we come up with some workable solutions.
- I don't get angry with someone who makes a huge error in judgment the first time. The second time the same person makes the same error, I get angry, but the anger doesn't last long. The third time, I get angry and make no apologies.
- You've been abusive to me and abusive to my customers. We don't tolerate that here. I no longer want your business.

Voicing Your Disagreement

In negotiation and conflict resolution, it's important that both sides are able to state their points of disagreement constructively, clearly, and precisely. You may not be able to control how others do this, but you can control how you voice your disagreements. Note that disagreement does not necessarily entail anger. Keep in mind that two well-intentioned, honorable people can disagree on issues.

- I understand what you're saying, Bob. Here are the points where we seem to differ ...

- Well, I do agree with you on most of your points, but I want to hear more about [insert details], because here's how I see the situation.

- I feel that your solution isn't going to take care of all of our problems.

- I think your proposal is a good one; but here's what I think we need to do as well.

- I want to agree with you on this, but we are forgetting one important aspect of the issue that I don't feel we've addressed yet.

- I'm sorry that's how you feel, Greta. It may seem like I'm favoring Lloyd over you, but he seems to have a more complete view of the situation at this point.

- This seems like such a simple problem, doesn't it? Let me discuss some other relevant issues with you to see if you agree that we need to look at them.

- I understand you think the error was at our end, and there's no doubt that's part of it, but I think we both have some responsibility regarding the delays, so let's talk about that.

Ethical Tough Negotiations

Often it's best to negotiate based on the premise that you and the other party can eventually cooperate and come to a mutually acceptable arrangement or solution. However, that's not always realistic. Sometimes it's appropriate or even optimal to negotiate tough, which involves presenting a colder and almost aggressive position—a tougher position in which your primary goal is to get what you want. Do not engage in personal attacks. Stick to the issues under negotiation. By avoiding personal attacks, you will be far more likely to maintain reasonable working relationships, even though you are negotiating tough.

- We've been trying to make this deal with you for weeks. If we don't come to an agreement today, we're looking elsewhere and the deal is off the table.

- Jack, I can't give you a 20 percent raise. I can give you a final offer of 5 percent this year and 5 percent next year. If that's not sufficient, then we'll have to end our relationship.

- Here's our final offer. No haggling, no more negotiating.

- It's not acceptable that delivery has been late the last two months. The next time delivery is late, we'll terminate our standing order.

- Come back with your best proposal, including the best quote you can offer. We aren't negotiating after that point; we'll either accept your proposal or refuse it.

- You aren't offering us anything that we can't get from 10 other businesses. Why should we deal with you specifically?

- This deal is off the table if you cannot agree to deliver my weekly order by Monday mornings at 7:30.

Stating and Drafting Final Agreements

Whether we're talking about concluding a complex business deal or completing some simple negotiation about employee salary, at some point there needs to be some statement of agreement, either written or oral and in either formal contract language or less formal. Sometimes a final statement of agreement may be drafted by both parties and sometimes by one or the other. Here are some phrases that fit various kinds of final agreements.

- Both parties have agreed that when the reports are delivered late, there is no adverse impact on the subsequent tasks that are performed with the reports. The process descriptions must be updated to reflect a later delivery date that is acceptable to both parties.
- The job schedules that produce the data for the reports will be examined to determine if the jobs can be started earlier in order to meet the monthly reporting deadline.
- Both supplier and customers will meet to formalize a communication process so that the supplier is available during the business day.
- The supplier has agreed to look for manufacturing problems that may cause problems.
- The supplier has agreed to take steps to improve its quality control processes.
- Joe and Gerald's immediate supervisor will review past assignments to assess the validity of Joe's claim.
- Mary and Anne's immediate supervisor will review their past performances to address Mary's concern.

- I agree that you deserve a raise. Starting July 3, your salary will be increased by 7 percent. The weekly rate will be [insert number].

- To be clear, John, we have a verbal handshake agreement that we'll start our consulting work with you on August 8th and that we will be billing you at an hourly rate of $100. I'll draft the final letter of agreement and get it to you this week. Is that OK?

- Mary, I know your company has some strict guidelines about the wording of contracts. We don't have so many legal requirements for our documents. So how about you draft the document and get it approved by your legal department, and then I'll look at it?

Guiding Principles

Conflict and disagreement are inevitable whenever two or more people or businesses interact. Differing positions need not be a bad thing, since conflict can lead to negotiation, which can, in turn, lead to creative, win-win solutions that would not have occurred otherwise.

Conflict can actually improve long-term relationships, provided you deal with it constructively and avoid making disagreements personal. Stick to issues. Avoid attacking people.

Firm negotiating tactics are sometimes necessary when the other party is using those same tactics or has been uncooperative over time. However, negotiating tough does not mean making personal attacks.

Successful negotiating requires clear communication so both sides understand each other's position and perspective and know each other's needs and wants.

Chapter 17
Hiring and Using Professionals

As a business owner and operator, you have strengths, weaknesses, and areas of expertise. There are also areas where you need assistance. Small business owners rely on the expertise of outsiders, since small enterprises don't have a full-time need for some kinds of expertise. It's more economical to hire expertise as it is required. It makes no sense to employ a full-time graphic artist when there are too few tasks for that person to do. Similarly you may not need a full-time certified public accountant or a full-time Web site developer. You can hire them as needed.

In this chapter we'll look at the things you need to consider when hiring and using professionals in some specific areas of need.

First, here are a few questions to ask anyone you may be thinking of hiring on a temporary basis.

- Can you provide examples of your work?
- Can you provide references for your work?

- How long have you been in business?
- What guarantees or warranties do you provide?
- How readily available are you for me if I experience problems with your product or service—including outside the hours of the traditional workweek?

Bankers

Bankers can be critically important to a small business, particularly if the business requires investment, loans, and other financing. Even if your business is not reliant on bank financing, your bank may be helpful in other ways, such as maximizing your interest on accounts, minimizing interest payments, and easing the process of moving money around. Banks don't just dispense money. They dispense business advice that can be very valuable if you choose to listen. Consequently, it's always a good idea to find a banker with whom you can communicate comfortably and get to know so you can create a long-term, personal relationship if that's possible.

You also need to get information from your banker about banking services, procedures, rules, and protocols. Here are a number of questions that may help you deal most effectively with a banker.

- Could you explain the basic differences between your personal banking services and your small business banking services?
- Could you explain the differences between a loan and a credit line and how a small business might benefit from either?
- Could you explain the difference between an overdraft line of credit and a bank loan and how a small business might benefit from either?
- Is it a good business practice for me to use credit when I buy from my suppliers?

- Is equity funding a good way to obtain financing for my business?
- Would you recommend factoring/invoicing discounting as a way to raise capital?
- Is it a better practice for me to lease or buy the major capital items I need to run my business?
- Can you discuss the pros and cons related to selling shares of my business?
- Is obtaining a grant a good way to raise cash for my business?
- Can you share any tips for cash-flow management?
- As my banker, will you communicate regularly with me and share your worries about my business with me and show me how to correct the problems you have identified?
- What kind of financial advice can you provide to me?
- What action do you take if I cannot repay my loan?

Information Technology and Computer Professionals

These days almost all businesses rely to some degree on computers and information technology. Communication, handling of transactions, marketing, and tax and sales records—virtually everything you do depends on working computers. Technology problems mean losses of revenue and customers.

Few small business owners and operators have the skills or time to manage their computer systems, so they do what is needed when it is needed in a secure and reliable way. If you can't handle all of the information technology tasks yourself and can't hire someone full time, you can hire an outside person on a part-time or consulting (as-needed) basis. You can do the latter project by project.

In this section we'll provide you with phrases that can help you hire information technology help and communicate more effectively with computer professionals. They are broken down into categories.

OUTLINING THE PROBLEM OR ISSUE

When you deal with an IT person, one of his or her goals is to understand your problem. To help clarify and quantify your problem, you should be ready to discuss it in depth.

- This is why I think the problem exists.
- The problem exists because my business grew so quickly.
- When I started my business, I didn't think I would want to capture information about my customers and their purchases.

- I thought it would be OK to accept only cash or checks as payment.
- We never considered that our Web site would be so popular. Now it's so slow, we're losing customers.
- Nobody thought to consider we should have multiple backup strategies for our critical data.
- When we were smaller, we didn't feel the need to track customer data and information, but now we want to start a free electronic newsletter.
- We've had only one computer, but now that I have several employees, we need a computer for each one and a network so they can all communicate.

MENTIONING SOLUTIONS YOU USE OR HAVE TRIED

You may have tried to address the problems already or have a temporary solution in place. The computer professional will need to know what you are doing currently to deal with the problem.

- I keep a notebook that lists each purchase, the purchaser's name, and the items purchased.
- I sort of just keep it in my head what inventory I have on hand and when I should start to restock.
- When a customer wants to use a credit card to make a purchase, I explain that I accept only cash or a check. I may lose the sale, or the customer will pay me in cash or by check.
- Once a week, I simply copy all of my financial and customer data onto a set of DVDs and put them in a drawer.
- I use Excel to keep track of my customers.
- I set up a home network kind of thing, but I don't think it's secure, and it doesn't seem that reliable.

EXPLAINING HOW OFTEN THE PROBLEM OCCURS AND WHO IS AFFECTED

Anyone you hire to resolve problems via the use of technology will need to know how serious the problems are, how they interfere with business, and how often.

- This is a problem for me only at month-end whenever I want to make a report about the type of sales made.

- At least once a week I have to tell a customer that his or her order will take up to two weeks to deliver.

- Almost daily I have customers who would prefer to buy using credit.

- My customers are not willing to wait; they want to take their purchases home right then.

- I am losing customers.

- The call center personnel have to deal with angry or abusive customers.

EXPLAINING THE COST OF THE PROBLEM

The cost of the problem quantifies the urgency and magnitude of the business impact. Cost includes lost business, lost customers, staff turnover, delays that affect revenue, and, of course, actual direct financial loss.

- I have calculated that I spend at least 20 extra hours a month preparing a manual report.

- Last week, I lost a $3,500 sale because I cannot accept credit card payments.

- Call center staff turnover is high, so I spend time, money, and effort recruiting new personnel.

- Delays as a result of slow computer responses have caused callers to hang up and customers to walk out.

COMMUNICATING ANY CONSTRAINTS AND REQUIREMENTS

When you hire someone, you never give that person carte blanche, freedom to do whatever he or she chooses. It's your business, and you have to communicate to the consultant any constraints or requirements for the solution. Communicate these as early in the hiring process as possible, and find out whether the consultant hire feels comfortable working within the constraints.

- The new system needs to be implemented by year-end.
- The cost of resolving the problem can be no more than $50,000.
- The new system must provide monthly data to my client payment system.
- Expert personnel will be available to you during this process for only an hour each day to answer questions about our current system.
- Your solution must comply with government-specified regulations.
- Your solution must be compatible with my desktop and laptop computers.

Suppliers

If you work with suppliers, you need to be able to communicate with them, assess them, and choose them efficiently and accurately. If you choose an unreliable supplier, you may have nothing to provide to your customers, or you may not be able to keep promises to your customers if the supplier cannot keep his or her promises to you.

- What sort of quality control processes do you have in place to ensure the quality of your products?
- What sort of troubleshooting process do you have in place to investigate complaints about your products and customer service?
- Do you provide rush order delivery?
- What are your order delivery methods?
- Is it your policy to keep customers informed of changes to your current products?
- Is it your policy to keep your customers informed of new products they may be interested in knowing about?
- How do you keep your prices competitive?
- Are you interested in knowing if I find a similar product at a lower price?
- Do you expect payment at delivery of supplies?
- Do your employees sign a confidentiality agreement with regard to their knowledge of my business as a result of my customers?
- How much lead time do you give your customers when you plan to raise your prices?

Marketing and Advertising

You may think you know a lot about marketing and advertising, because you see it everyday. Below the surface of any successful marketing or advertising campaign is a great deal of specialized knowledge and skills that went into making the campaign a success. For this reason you might want to retain an advertising professional on a freelance or project basis. This may allow you to learn from him or her, in addition to getting a jump-start on marketing your business. Here are some phrases that can guide you when you go hunting for marketing and advertising help.

- Tell me about any awards you have received for your work.
- What do you think has been your most innovative marketing campaign to date and why?
- What do you think has been your least memorable marketing campaign to date and why?
- What questions do you have regarding my business?
- Tell me what sets you apart from other marketing and advertising experts.
- Do you have statistics that prove that your marketing and advertising efforts have been beneficial to your clients?
- What do you think your current clients think about working with you?
- What do you think past clients would tell me about working with you?
- Tell me about your payment structure. Do you charge according to proven results or service rendered?

- How do you decide how to tackle creating a marketing campaign?
- How do you decide you want to work with a client?
- Have you ever fired a client? If so, why?
- Have you ever left a client? If so, why?
- Do you typically work for small businesses?

Accounting Help

All businesses must keep appropriate records, particularly financial ones, and keep them in good order and according to normally accepted practices. The smaller your business and the less complex, the less you need a high-level expert to do your books. However, accounting help is not limited to simple bookkeeping. An accountant who specializes in small businesses can be a huge asset by advising you on how to optimize your revenues, save on taxes, and make use of capital.

- How many clients do you currently represent?
- What is the average length of time you have been representing them?
- Do any of your clients own a small business similar to mine? If yes, please tell me if you see this as a potential conflict of interest. If you don't perceive a conflict of interest, please explain to me why not.
- Tell me how you keep current with technology that can help small businesses.
- What is your professional designation?
- What provisions do you make, such as hiring extra personnel, to ensure meeting my business needs during the busy tax season?
- Can you advise me about what kind of business entity I should form and the reasons for your recommendation?
- Can you advise me about financing my company and the reasons for doing so or not doing so?
- How much do you know about my type of business or industry?

- How quickly can you adapt to changes in my organization?
- How often can I expect accounting and financial reports?
- Can I expect you to remind me of due dates for reports and taxes?
- What are the tax advantages to leasing the major capital items I need to run my business?
- What are the tax advantages to buying the major capital items I need to run my business?
- Tell me how you keep updated with the current tax laws applicable to small business.

Training and Education

It's to everyone's benefit to ensure that the people in your business, including yourself, stay current and continue to develop relevant skills. Sometimes learning can occur from sharing internally, but it's often the case that it's more economical or more practical for an employee to attend training or take advantage of relevant educational options outside of your company.

However, before you finalize arrangements for training or education, get enough information from the vendor or provider about the particular training event or course so you can determine if it will fulfill your business needs. Here are some phrases to use to find out what you should know.

- Describe for me your process of delivering education to business—from the initial client contact forward.
- How do you measure and evaluate the effectiveness of your training sessions?
- What would you say is your strongest attribute as a trainer?
- Tell me how you keep yourself current as a business trainer.
- Do you do one-on-one training?
- Tell me about actions you would take in the workshop to encourage participation when it is obvious that the participants are unwilling.
- Tell me about your adult training credentials.
- Would you sign a confidentiality agreement with regard to details of my business?

- Do you customize your training workshops?
- Have you ever discouraged a potential client from hiring you? Tell me about the circumstances.
- Before you begin to plan your training session, I would like you to create a needs assessment document. Describe to me the typical questions that would be asked of the participants.
- Tell me what you consider to be the biggest misconception about business training and education.

Insurance Companies and Representatives

As is the case with hiring other professionals, insurance companies and representatives serve two functions. The first is to provide you with insurance, of course. The second is to provide advice about what kinds of insurance you require and advice on the best choices among the options available. That means you need to create a relationship with your "insurance person" based on trust.

Here are some phrases to help you get to know your insurance agent and how he or she can help you. If the insurance agent answers your questions in ways that suggest his or her only interest is making a commission, go elsewhere until you find one that seems to express both an interest in your business and a concern about your welfare.

- Tell me how I can reduce my insurance payments and still maintain adequate insurance coverage.
- Are there standard preferred business security systems that I can use to lower my insurance payments?
- How does the insurance industry define "small business"?
- Tell me about the coverage of a standard insurance policy for a small business.
- How do I make an insurance claim?
- What is the best kind of insurance coverage for my business?
- How familiar are you with my type of small business?
- Is there some extra coverage a business like mine should carry?

- Should my company car be insured under my small business policy or under my personal policy?
- Are there some common business practices I should be following in order to qualify for small business insurance?
- Do I need to take a medical exam in order to qualify for small business insurance?
- Would life insurance be automatically included in my small business insurance policy?
- Would health and dental insurance be automatically included in my small business insurance policy?
- Is the small business owner's age a factor in insurance costs?

Legal Counsel

Even if you don't foresee needing a lawyer, chances are that at some point you will require one for routine work (such as evaluating a contract) or major work (such as dealing with a potential lawsuit). It's not a bad idea to start building a long-term relationship with legal counsel even if you don't have an immediate need for his or her services. That way, when you need the service, the lawyer will be familiar with you and your business. If hiring a lawyer is a new experience for you, you might want to talk with other small business owners who have hired counsel.

Here are a few phrases you can use when talking with a lawyer to evaluate whether there's a fit between you and him or her and whether you are comfortable with the person.

- Tell me about your billing guidelines or policies.
- I plan to sell my business and need help with setting a realistic price.
- I am expanding my business into another state and need to know about any legal ramifications.
- Is there a checklist of activities related to business in general that require legal counsel?
- Tell me about any legal pitfalls that seem prevalent within my type of business.
- Tell me about any legal pitfalls that seem prevalent within any small business.
- Once I end our attorney-client relationship with your legal firm, what happens to my file?
- I have created an advertisement and marketing campaign for my small business. Do I need legal counsel to review it?

Guiding Principles

You can't do everything on your own. While it may seem wasteful to spend money on professionals for tasks you believe you can do yourself, keep in mind that investing to have something done right is often way cheaper than doing it inadequately. Professionals are simply more likely to do things properly.

Even if you don't have an immediate need for the kinds of professionals listed in this chapter, consider forming relationships with such professionals, with an eye to the long term. It really helps to be prepared before you have a crisis or major project that requires immediate help.

The professionals listed here provide a service or product (e.g., loans, insurance policies, tax preparation, training, computer technology, and so on), but it's just as important to recognize that they can provide essential advice in their areas of expertise. Ask for the advice. Listen to the advice. Don't let pride stand in the way of getting the most benefit from the experts you are paying.

Chapter 18
Reporting on the Business and Working with Financial Investors/Partners

N o business is an island. No matter how small your business, there will likely be times when you need to report
on the state of your business and/or approach others
for investment. You may need to communicate with family
members and other potential investors. This chapter deals with
some of these situations—communicating with others on the
status of your business.

Annual Reports

Depending on your circumstances (e.g., business entity, type of investors, laws in your state), you may be obligated to file an annual report. In other circumstances, you may not be obligated to write a report, but should do so. For example, if you have family and friends who have invested in your business, you may not be required to furnish an annual report, but it would certainly be professional and correct to do so. Even if your business is a sole proprietorship, it's useful to do an annual report for yourself, so you can see exactly where you've been and commit to paper where you are going in the future.

When preparing an annual report for public consumption, it's wise to consult legal counsel and an accountant. This can help you conform to legal and accounting standards requirements and keep you out of trouble. Here is some very basic information about the content and phrasing of annual reports.

FOR THE REPORTING PERIOD

- Reporting period date
- Mission and purpose of your company
- Statement of income showing how much money your company made during your reporting year
- Cash-flow statement showing how your company pays for its day-to-day operations and future expansion
- Balance sheet listing what your company owns and owes
- Any other financial information required by accounting practices

- State of the market (expanding, contracting, etc.)
- Changes in market share, profit margins
- Explanations of major changes in revenue

FOR THE NEXT REPORTING PERIOD

- Projections for next reporting period
- Plans to remedy negative results from current reporting period
- Plans to expand or alter business directions
- Projections for additional needed investment
- Projections for return on investment

KEY QUESTIONS TO CONSIDER BEFORE WRITING THE ANNUAL REPORT

- Who will be receiving my annual report (investors, financiers, others)?
- What are their major concerns? How must I address them in the report?
- Do I have sufficient information to do the annual report? If not, how do I get missing information?
- Do I have reasonable explanations for where we have been during the last year and why?
- Do I have reasonable explanations for where we are going in the next year and why?
- Whom will I get to review the annual report before it is ready to go?

Raising Money from Family and Friends

Owners of start-up businesses often look to family and friends to finance them until they get on their feet. That's usually because banks or other investors have refused requests for credit or loans. Having investors from your personal circle can be awkward. Unless you handle those relationships well, you can be risking extreme acrimony and loss of friends or alienation of family members. Here are some phrases that you should consider when recruiting investors from your personal circle and communicating with them.

- We should discuss what may happen to our relationship if my business fails.
- We should discuss what may happen to our relationship if my business succeeds beyond the projections documented in my business plan.
- Here is the schedule I'm proposing for paying off the loan and interest.
- This is a loan that I will repay to you with interest; it does not mean that you own any part of my business.
- I will provide you with a document stating how much money I have borrowed from you.
- If at any time you wish to pull your money out of my company, I will return it immediately.
- I want to treat this as a business transaction rather than a personal one, so let's follow all the rules and do all the documentation as if we were strangers.
- It's important to me that you don't invest any more than you can lose. I don't think you'll lose anything, but there's always a risk.

Talking with Prospective Investors

When asking people to invest in your business, keep in mind two things. You want something from the other party, but you are also offering an opportunity to the other party. Treat potential investors appropriately. Be neither too eager nor "easy" or arrogant, expecting unrealistic terms. The best investment discussions end with both parties feeling they succeeded. To that end, try to make sure the investor's interests align with your own. Here are some phrases you can use when talking with potential investors.

- I am interested in running a "green" company, despite the added expenses.
- I am interested in retaining control of my company and will not give up more than 49 percent of it.
- I can guarantee you a return on your investment within five years.
- I cannot guarantee that your investment is a short-term investment.
- Accepting your investment money is conditional on your agreeing with my long-term goals as outlined in my business plan.
- Would you be willing to introduce me to some potential customers?
- Can I also rely on you for financial advice, if I need it in the future?
- What are your hopes regarding return on your investment?
- As part owner, how much are you expecting to be involved in day-to-day operations?

- How does your investment fit in with your other business enterprises?
- Besides the financial conditions, what other information do you need to increase your investment in our business?
- What concerns do you have about how we run the company?
- How can we reassure you about how business decisions will be made?

Negotiating a Loan

For many people the process of negotiating a loan is intimidating and downright scary. It can feel a bit like being a kid in school asking the principal for a favor. Keep in mind that, as with recruiting investors, you are asking for something while offering something in return (payment of interest on the loan). The lender will benefit if everything works out as you hope. Loans are not charity. They are business propositions. Act accordingly. This is no time for any arrogance or blatant in-your-face bluster about the value of your business.

Below are questions you should have a banker answer when you are negotiating a loan. The questions are followed by several checklists.

- Is the interest rate negotiable?
- In addition to the interest rate, how much is this loan really costing me?
- Will I be charged any additional fees when I borrow money?
- Am I required to make any deposit in order to secure a loan?
- If I pay off my loan early, will I have to pay a penalty?
- Can I make bigger payments than scheduled without penalty? If so, how often?
- Can you explain the different interest rate types applicable to business loans?
- Can you explain the different business loans available to me?

- Other than ensuring that I pay my loan back, how else would you be involved in my business?
- What kind of reporting would you provide to me about my loan?
- What kind of reporting would you expect from me?
- What kinds of equity/security are required?

CHECKLIST—REASONABLE LOAN CONDITIONS

❑ Discuss events other than failure to repay the loan on time that the lender deems a "default."

❑ Discuss a reasonable grace period for your repayment schedule so that late payment charges are not invoked.

❑ Ensure that late payment charges are reasonable.

❑ Ensure that the collateral requested by the lender is reasonable.

CHECKLIST OF DOCUMENTS TO BRING TO YOUR FIRST MEETING WITH A LENDER

❑ Business profile that describes your business, including how big it is, who owns it, and when it started

❑ Business plan that describes your business's key objectives, goals, and initiatives

❑ Loan request, a document that tells how much money you would like to borrow and how you will use it in your business

❑ List of collateral to document any assets you currently own and are willing to use as collateral

❑ Your business and personal financial statements to provide an accurate overview of your current financial status

Talking with Prospective Partners

There are some benefits to owning and operating a business in partnership with another person or a company. These benefits may start with tax savings and extend right through to the synergy that can come from having two highly motivated owners working together to come up with better ideas for succeeding.

However, partnerships have drawbacks. Their success has a lot to do with the suitability and compatibility of the partners and the extent to which each partner is willing to compromise and work cooperatively. Unfortunately, when business partnerships fail, the financial and emotional fallout can be quite severe, much like what happens when a marriage fails.

Here are some phrases and questions to consider, starting with determining if you, in fact, are suited to run a business in a partnership.

- Do I prefer to work alone?
- Would I resent having to make business decisions with a partner?
- Can I deal with the frustration and slowdown of having to consult my business partner on all major decisions?
- What aspects of the business am I willing to relinquish to accommodate a partner's skills, abilities, and desires?

Here are some questions to consider when evaluating a particular potential business partner.

- Do I trust this person?
- Do we communicate well with each other during good

times and stressful times?

- Do we communicate well when we don't share the same opinions?
- Are our work ethics similar?
- Does this person understand and support the business plan?
- Do our personalities and business skills complement each other?
- Do we have a history of successful conflict resolution?
- Am I comfortable that our goals for the business are similar, both short and long term?

Here are some phrases to initiate discussion with a prospective business partner.

- Here's what I expect from you as a business partner ...
- Can you describe what you expect from me as a business partner?
- Here's how I think partnering with you can make this business better ...
- Here are the qualities I most admire about you as a businessperson ...
- Here are the qualities I most admire about you personally ...
- Are you willing to sign a legal agreement about our partnership?
- How will we go about solving disagreements and conflict?
- If we come to an unresolvable impasse, how can we terminate the partnership fairly and with as little rancor as possible?
- What are your goals for the business for the first year?
- Where do you see the business going in five years?

- Do you want to expand, or are you content with the size of the business?
- Are you in this for the long haul?

Communicating About Company Performance

Apart from the annual report, you will want to remain prepared to communicate about the performance of your business. Even if you are a sole owner, you need performance information at least monthly so you are able to make changes in the way you are running your business. Fast response is a major advantage of small business, and the key to making fast responses is to monitor performance, analyze it, and take action quickly.

Below is a list of the kinds of things you should track, for yourself and for others. You'll note that these are also elements that would be included in an annual report.

- Total sales revenues are ...
- Total sales costs are ...
- Total operating expenses are ...
- Total net cash from operations is ...
- Total net cash from financing is ...
- Total cash assets are ...
- Total equipment assets are ...
- Total accounts payable are ...
- Total debts are ...

Guiding Principles

When asking for a loan or an investment, remember that you are asking for something in return for something. You are hoping to receive something by offering some benefit. Loans and investments are opportunities for both parties.

When discussing loans and investments, do not project an arrogant attitude. Despite what you may think, your business idea is probably not the best thing since sliced bread. Be realistic. Be honest. Listen. Even if your request is declined, you may learn from the discussions and learn about weaknesses in your business plan, idea, or presentation.

Investments from family and friends are often a last resort. Be aware that the risks extend beyond financial ones. Many families have been ruptured by failed joint business endeavors and many friendships damaged. Just because you have great friends or great family members does not mean you should do business with them or request money from them.

Owning a business in partnership can bring about incredible benefits due to the synergy and motivation that can occur when two or more motivated and differentially skilled people are running a business. It's also a structure fraught with challenges and difficulties, so take care not to get caught up in the initial buzz and excitement of working with a partner. It's much like a marriage. Excitement isn't enough. Explore the issues before committing to a business partnership.